A Man of Faith Next Door

Written By: Paul E. Abbott

Copyright

Published: 19 January 2019

ISBN #: 978-1-71679-214-4

Copyright © 2019 by The Forge Foundation

585 6th Avenue Troy, New York 12182

www.theforgefoundation.org

Table of Contents

Amorío / Silent Vociferation

α. Staring at the Sun

Pro Sacrificial Laudis / Fidelity

β. The Beautiful & The Damned

Souvenirs Malléables / Anointed

δ. Raspberry Jammed

 Interludes I-XVII

Ab Initio / Desolation

ε. Gevind en Verlore

Exitium / Respite

ζ. Who is my neighbor?

Deditio / Amalgamation

η. Discouraged

Indebted / Seclusion

θ. Resurrected by Love

Mom, where do weddings come from? / Ruina

ι. Iter Usque Ad Ultimum Terra

I dedicate this book to my goddaughter Isabella.

"Elephants don't know anything about the world of ants; The peaks of mountains are oblivious of what is happening on the plains."

-Mehemet Murat ildan

Amorío

Insatiable love.

It broke me.

I will not have just any body.

A one-sided love affair.

Temptations plentiful.

Convincing commitments that last for never.

I never ran out on love.

But I struggled to remain the Man of Faith Next Door.

Silent Vociferation

I sincerely urge you to begin looking at what God has made us as His people through His word.

It is my devotion to research and convey the concepts of faith through all teachings in hopes to draw His children closer to Him, whichever way they choose to walk.

I would like to start in the New Testament scriptures, particularly Ephesians, to illustrate the premise that God had - in His grace - poured His blessings onto us.

It is something that is profound and unique in the New Testament scriptures.

It emits the idea that God intends us to grow, build and flourish.

"For we are God's handiwork, created in Christ Jesus to do good works, which God prepared in advance for us to do." Ephesians 2:10

So, what are these 'handiworks' in which God pre-equipped us to do?

We found that good works is followed by good success, and that is what God desires of us.

Because bad success is also possible and prevalent.

And what is equivalent to good works?

To serve His purposes - to spread His word of

redemption.

How do we bring redemption?

By bringing His word wherever we go!

But our influence and impact are only as strong as our character.

Can others believe and trust in the good news that you bring?

Do you show that the good news and good works have made a change in and with your own life before you begin to try and speak of them?

Consider Jesus:

What exactly made Him stand out?

He was an ordinary person, like you or me.

What made Him stand out was His obedience to the Father and His empowerment by the Spirit.

His godly character made a difference to those He met.

His actions changed them.

Jesus carried Himself in a way that projected the presence of God in every aspect.

We are all children of God, and we should aspire to walk in the room and radiate righteousness, such as Jesus did.

If we are to be a people who plan to work Gods purposes, then we will need to reflect the divine character.

"Grace and peace be yours in abundance through the knowledge of God and of Jesus our Lord. His divine power has given us everything we need for a godly life through our knowledge of Him who called us by His own glory and goodness." **2 Peter 1:2-3**

We are called to be godly, and most importantly:

He *empowers* us to do it.

Peter's words insist that God expects and equips us for godly living, and He gives us His promise to back it up.

"Through these He has given us His very great and precious 'promises, so that through them you may participate in the divine nature, having escaped the corruption in the world caused by evil desires." **2 Peter 1:4**

We see that Jesus died to deal with sin and the consequences of sin and what we have come into by faith is that we have

"...escaped the corruption in the world caused by evil desires."

We have been equipped with everything we require to participate in godly living.

To be righteously divine because that is what God wants of us.

Which leaves us with some awkward questions as His people.

Do we reflect the divine character?

This phrase is a really challenging statement.

We have come to rejoice and celebrate for everything that God has blessed us with and allowed us to overcome.

But have we *escaped* them?

Do we feel free from that which we were once bound by?

Things that were pronounced dead in your life showed back up the next day.

We are past worrying about smoking cigarettes and skipping church - but what about the systems in your life that hinder you from being the strongest, healthiest, and best possible version of yourself?

One of the most critical hindrances that people of faith have when it comes to leading others to God is not that they are unable or unwilling to open their mouth to tell others the good news – they are quick enough to do that believe me – but their lives just don't show it.

What do people see when they see you?

Do you live the passion you preach?

What do they receive and gain when they see you?

What do they hear?

Do you inspire others to believe?

Or are you selectively and mostly gracious.

Whatever your answer, Peter's answer is that we should be a godly people.

Even more significant, that we participate in the divine nature.

"And because of His glory and excellence, He has given us great and precious promises. These are the promises that enable you to share His divine nature and escape the world's corruption caused by human desires."

So, what character does a godly life, and a partaker of the divine nature entail?

Peter gives us this interesting list that leads to our growth as people of faith.

What he says is that we need to make contributions.

Peter is talking about adding to our faith.

God wants to contribute to our faith so that we may have everything we need to live a godly life so we can participate in the divine nature.

So, what needs to be added to our faith to turn us into what God wants of us and which decisions will allow us to be the people He desires us to be?

"For this very reason, make every effort to add to your faith."

We should enthusiastically desire to contribute generously in order to participate in the divine nature.

Do our intentions show that?

So, what do we add to our faith so that we can become the strongest conduit of the word of God to relay and spread to other people?

GODLINESS

The Greek word used here (Eusebia) is another word rarely used in the New Testament which refers more to reverence than godliness.

It does not refer to the masked-outward appearance that religious people like to put on - but a practical awareness of God in every aspect of life.

UNDERSTANDING

As we grow, evolve, and even begin to convey deeds of trust - we acquire knowledge and understanding.

We get to know what is good and bad, what's right and wrong, because walking with God, we understand what truth is because He is the truth.

We become wise as He is wise.

GOODNESS

This word is not a common New Testament word.

It is a Greek word used in secular circles to infer excellence.

The sense is that the desire we should have is to be the best.

Peter used this word to describe God:

"He has called us by His own glory and goodness."

What we should be adding is the excellence of God in our lives and in the community.

It reinforces the challenge we have already mentioned.

Goodness is practical because, just as Jesus touched people's lives and changed them, so we are called to be life-changers.

Before you see yourselves short or accept that you are only human; remember we have the divine power within us.

TEMPERANCE

This is not merely about controlling ourselves in terms of what we eat, what we drink, what we spend, or how we act - but how much of our ego we desire to project.

As we acquire knowledge, we see that self-control is control of selfishness and putting the needs of others before ourselves.

Temperance has obedience and humility at its heart, and that is the very nature of God.

How do I know that?

"The Lord Jesus Christ who, being in very nature God, did not consider equality with God something to be used to His own advantage; rather, He made himself nothing by taking the very nature of a servant, being made in human likeness. And being found in appearance as a man, He humbled Himself by becoming obedient to death— even death on a

cross!"

He became obedient unto death.

The greatest humility is obedience and losing our own desire to think like the rest of the world.

PERTINACITY

The next addition builds from self-control as we seek to build a character and live a faithful life - and we find it is not easy.

The way of obedience for Jesus was not nearly as simple as these items tell us.

Being humble, godly, and all the latter is not always appreciated inside the church - and outside it can be described as the temper of mind which is unmoved by difficulty or distress.

If you want to be godly, the enemy attacks us, the world attacks us.

The faithful life is not easy.

We are fortunate for the unity we have in most of our communities: it is a value we should persevere with.

FELLOWSHIP

As John puts it in his first letter; we cannot say we love God and hate our brother (or sister).

One of the most painful things to deal with is ministering in an environment where there's hostility and not affection.

As God's people, this one is important today where politics have become more aggressive.

Simply, people lack respect for one another.

Here's how Michael Green describes brotherly kindness:

"Love for the brethren entails bearing one another's burdens, and so fulfilling the law of Christ: it means guarding that Spirit-given unity from destruction by gossip, prejudice, narrowness, and the refusal to accept a brother Christian for what he is in Christ."

Peter makes it more difficult by amplifying that with his last word.

LOVE

Unconditional; Agape; always putting others before ourselves.

He wants us to cultivate the quality of love in ourselves.

It is what sums up the foregoing.

When we take it seriously, it is what really marks us out as being different.

What we do can and does make a difference to lives and help bring someone closer to God by witnessing the faithful and outworking spirit evolve in our very own lives.

It is feeling the presence of God when they experience church.

It is what gives us a passion for the word of God.

Passion for our faith.

NOTES

Staring at the Sun

As an adolescent, I was most comfortable in solitude and isolated myself as often as possible.

I did not talk until I was about seven or eight years old.

In the years to come, I would not speak unless provoked with questions or emotionally crippling banter.

Others thought that I was quiet because I was content.

Incidentally, I was flinching.

I always felt as if I was backed into a corner and surrounded by a barrage of people as they mocked, ostracized, and berated my faith-filled intentions and self-sovereignty.

So, I locked myself away and allowed my determination and character to deteriorate for most of my childhood.

Although, even during the attack launched against myself, I was always known by friends and family to be extremely adaptable, tenacious, and reverential.

I have always been accepting of alternative perspectives and often sought after them in hopes to fulfill my infatuation of understanding the mysteries of life, but mostly in an attempt to repair my malfunctioning heart.

I never really could escape the fact that I felt miserable or alone with company and whole by myself.

Even in mediocre conversation, my heart begins to attack me.

Over time I have grown accustom to the constant torture and habitually clench my jaw tight while I bottle the brewing intensity of a whirlwind of emotions.

I could tear the paint off the walls and scream until my lips turned blue, but not even the person next to me nor the person who loved me the most could hear.

Driven, but perplexed, I grew to experience the frivolous and unequivocally putrid matters of my own despair and tragedy ridden life.

I could always envision the silver lining in its mendacity and lucid absence.

Against the constant strain of my heart I have always had unconditional love for the world, along with the strangest of strangers, while simultaneously fighting the urge and even the opportunity to live the rest of my days in detrimental acrimony.

From the beginning, I was mandated to consistently and effortlessly confide my heart and soul into the individuals that cross my path and come to surround me.

I was dually mandated to clear the way for those behind me and to endure the thorns for the faith to carry on protected in love.

Guarded by only those who claim love as a commandment, a commitment, and a privilege.

Until there is no love unseen, unheard, or unfed.

I recognize my purpose to derive from the support from my friends and family which allowed me to experience trust and love regardless of what happened before and the perilous perspective I have of it all.

Reflecting on my memories with them led to the transformation of my perception and I was turned faithful to the individuals who would come to enter and exit my life, customarily and often emphatically in haste.

I was also turned faithful to my family during times of our struggles and distressed circumstances rather than foolishly, childishly, and selfishly rebelling against their attempts to care for me through their own tests and trials.

But most of all I was turned once again faithful to God, and for always remembering Him, He has always remembered me.

I could never be alone, no matter how hard I tried.

That is not to say that I have been or always will be wise or have the strength to overcome the obstacles before me at any given point in time.

However, I have grown in every aspect.

I was able learn invaluable lessons from each and

every travesty.

That is also not to say that I have always been supported or had clear directions to help get me through the chaos or received protection against the presence and advances from the enemy.

Instead, I was given moments with individuals as my turning points, directing me towards my destiny and inscribing divine signals within my unconscious nerves.

One thing I am not sure of is whether I have always believed in religion.

Surely, there was a time in my life where I did not believe in myself, as there were many nights that I stayed awake just because I did not want to wake up the next day.

Despite disbelief in myself, I have always believed there was somebody listening to the silent screams of the worried little boy inside of the man that I grew up to be.

Belief in that alone gave me the comfort not to worry all night, and faith gave me the courage to rise in the morning with my head up and my back straight.

When I came to realize that my loneliness, anxiety, fear, doubts, and insecurities were only doors to be opened with my granted preparation or down time as the key, I was unable to push past even the least hindering limitations.

Unfortunately, I had to be forced to reach down and find the strength and tenacity within my heart.

Fortunately, I was never the same person again.

I soon convinced myself that I had the power to simply speak and I began to share my thoughts finding a deeper relation to even the strangest of strangers.

I would never again let my emotions hold me back from at least trying to complete even the seemingly tepid challenges.

I believe it was at this exact time that I decided to suffer loudly the rest of my life if I had to live for a higher purpose and I made it a responsibility to sacrifice my integrity to inspire and influence others.

I only feel as though I received my flourishing blessings and prolific successes because my heart was truly in the right place even when my head was not.

I found that I had the capacity to love with purest adoration and to also endure the most afflicting pain and hardship.

From that point on I truly knew that God was guarding my heart as I opened it to the great unknown and allowed the unveilings of life's greatest moments, mysteries, and miseries to flow through my spirit.

Not deprived of the overwhelming frustration, and for His will to prosper above all of those around me and even my own expectations.

Emerging from the catacombs was not of my own power.

I was not spiritually sound, physically capable, intellectually astute, or emotionally stable in my season of miracles.

It was a result of my devotion that incited His will to strengthen my armor and empower my soul to prosper through hell and high water.

To understand more about ones' heart, you need to understand their experiences and the environment in which those experiences occurred along with the perspective in which they view their experience from.

I hope with indulging my most excruciating moments and my most consuming feelings that you will come to understand more about your values, and I hope my words will inspire you to rewrite your story if you have the audacity to change your perception and the will to begin the fight through all the exhausting emotions to reach His destiny for you.

It will not be easy, but what makes the character in your story and what creates the character of your personality and virtues are on completely different scales, and likely in differing perspectives.

Please read this with the understanding that this is not just a story, but a walking testimony of faith from the hollows of my very own heart that I confide to illustrate an eternally graceful premise,

"Faithful are the wounds of a friend." -<u>Proverbs 27:6</u>

"In the end, we will conserve only what we love, we will love all that we understand, and we will understand only what we are taught."

-Baba Dioum

Pro Sacrificial Laudis

I was incarcerated young.

A prisoner of this everlasting civil war.

Idolizing leaders corrupted by authority.

Malnourished in tradition.

Immersed in division.

I was freed through knowledge.

Now lost, but free.

Left wandering in search of all that I had lost.

Taking for granted all that I had left over.

I was held captive by my own demise.

A wandering prison.

I withered before it could be found.

Before I could find myself.

Fidelity

Ruth is a short, yet powerful book tucked among the Old Testaments.

Its events are in accordance with the book of Judges - set during a time when there was no king in Israel, and,

"Every man did what was right in his own eyes."
Judges 17:6

Warren Wiersbe spins it like this:

"The book of Judges is the story of Israel at one of its lowest points in history – it's a record of division, cruelty, apostasy, civil war, and national disgrace. Spiritually, our lives resemble elements of the book of Judges, for there is no king in Israel, and there will not be until Jesus returns. Like Israel in the past, many of God's people today are living in unbelief and disobedience and are not enjoying the blessings of God."

As we travel along the road between Moab (a picture of the world) and Bethlehem (God's city of promised blessing and the future birthplace of the Messiah), let us find rest in knowing Jesus traveled this road for us so that we could live an eternal life in His House of Praise.

The book of Ruth is a beautifully redeeming love story.

Although, its beginnings are rooted in tragedy.

This is a story about a family that makes one unwise decision out of fear - and in return receives three graves.

Fear drives unwise decisions.

"Now it came to pass, in the days when the judges ruled, that there was a famine in the land. And a certain man of Bethlehem, Judah, went to dwell in the country of Moab, he and his wife and his two sons. The name of the man was Elimelech, the name of his wife was Naomi, and the names of his two sons were Mahlon and Chilion—Ephrathites of Bethlehem, Judah. And they went to the country of Moab and remained there. Then Elimelech, Naomi's husband, died; and she was left, and her two sons. Now they took wives of the women of Moab: the name of the one was Orpah, and the name of the other Ruth. And they dwelt there about ten years. Then both Mahlon and Chilion also died; so the woman survived her two sons and her husband." Ruth 1:1-5

There was a famine in Bethlehem.

In Old Testament times, a famine was an outward display of God's judgement on His people because of their unbelief and disobedience.

"If my people, who are called by my name, will humble themselves and pray and seek my face and turn from their wicked ways, then I will hear from heaven, and I will forgive their sin and will heal their land."   2 Chronicles 7:14

When a famine hits our own heart, our encouragement from God is that we:

1.) Humble ourselves

2.) Pray for forgiveness.

3.) Seek His face.

4.) Change our direction.

And God's promise to us is that He will listen, forgive, and restore.

If you have a heart that is weighing you down today, take a moment to put into action what the Lord desires for your life:

Humble yourself.

Pray for forgiveness.

Fix your eyes.

Seek His face.

Embrace a new perspective.

Challenge your perception.

And change your direction.

One thing to note about the patriarch, Elimelech, is this:

He chose poorly for his family.

Instead of enduring the famine, he ran from his problems and chose to walk by sight and not by faith.

This exemplifies the moments in our lives where we

run away from God rather than run to Him.

Running away means that you choose to be comfortably numb and kin to a life beneath the promises of God – beneath the bountiful love and abundance of life that He offers.

Running to Him means that regardless of how you feel, what you see, or what may happen - you make a conscious decision to live on purpose.

Both those who run away and towards God are in the midst of turmoil – they are uncomfortable, and their emotions are exhausted.

Both even have hope that things will get brighter ahead – though only one has the radical faith to trust God.

"Then she arose with her daughters-in-law that she might return from the country of Moab, for she had heard in the country of Moab that the Lord had visited His people by giving them bread. Therefore, she went out from the place where she was, and her two daughters-in-law with her; and they went on the way to return to the land of Judah. And Naomi said to her two daughters-in-law, "Go, return each to her mother's house. The Lord deal kindly with you, as you have dealt with the dead and with me. The Lord grant that you may find rest, each in the house of her husband." So, she kissed them, and they lifted their voices and wept. And they said to her, "Surely we will return with you to your people." **Ruth 1:6-10**

Naomi was ready to return to her home country.

She had lost her husband and two sons in a foreign land.

However, take note that Naomi did not encourage her Moabite daughters-in-law to return with her to God's land.

Interesting move on her part.

If Naomi brought both of her daughters to Bethlehem with her, then the people would have realized she disobeyed God and departed from His will by not only leaving the Promise Land but marrying her sons off to a sinful nation.

When we cover up our poor decisions, it only creates more weight to carry.

1 John 1:9 assures us that if we confess our sins, He is faithful and just and will forgive us our sin and cleanse us from all wickedness.

I would rather have a cleansed heart than one I am trying to constantly cover up.

In this very moment, confess your poor decisions before the Lord and allow Him to heal your broken heart so you do not have a bitter one.

"But Naomi said, "Turn back, my daughters; why will you go with me? Are there still sons in my womb, that they may be your husbands? Turn back, my daughters, go—for I am too old to have a husband. If I should say I have hope, if I should have a husband tonight and should also bear sons, would you wait for them till they were grown? Would you restrain yourselves from having

husbands? No, my daughters; for it grieves me very much for your sakes that the hand of the Lord has gone out against me!" Then they lifted up their voices and wept again; and Orpah kissed her mother-in-law, but Ruth clung to her. And she said, "Look, your sister-in-law has gone back to her people and to her gods; return after your sister-in-law." But Ruth said: "Entreat me not to leave you, or to turn back from following after you; For wherever you go, I will go; and wherever you lodge, I will lodge; your people shall be my people, and your God, my God. Where you die, I will die, and there will I be buried. The Lord do so to me, and more also, if anything but death parts you and me." When she saw that she was determined to go with her, she stopped speaking to her." <u>Ruth 1:11-18</u>

Here we read both Orpah's and Ruth's response.

A parallel of how we ourselves respond to the Lord.

In Orpah's case, she started off to Bethlehem, but her actions proved that her heart was stuck back home in Moab.

While Ruth was a woman from a sinful land, yet she was willing to stand up and choose God and follow through with her actions.

Ruth's decision is a picture of God's grace.

Ruth was a Gentile woman who did not know the Lord.

Yet, despite her difficult trials and heartache, she clung to Naomi and was determined to accompany her.

Ruth's loyalty to Naomi is a parallel picture of how we are to respond to Christ by saying,

"I will not leave you, Lord. Wherever you go, I will go."

"Now the two of them went until they came to Bethlehem. And it happened, when they had come to Bethlehem, that all the city was excited because of them; and the women said, "Is this Naomi?" But she said to them, "Do not call me Naomi; call me Mara, for the Almighty has dealt very bitterly with me. I went out full, and the Lord has brought me home again empty. Why do you call me Naomi, since the Lord has testified against me, and the Almighty has afflicted me?" So Naomi returned, and Ruth the Moabitess her daughter-in-law with her, who returned from the country of Moab. Now they came to Bethlehem at the beginning of barley harvest." <u>Ruth 1:19-22</u>

Naomi had been away from Bethlehem for 10 years.

The people's question of,

"Is this Naomi?" was from both bewilderment and surprise.

Naomi's name means pleasant, but she told her people to call her Mara (which means bitter).

The same is true for us when we are out of fellowship with Him.

While sin may be pleasurable for a season (<u>Hebrews</u>

<u>11:25</u>), that season quickly withers, and we are left with repercussions and shame.

A life of sin brings a life of bitterness.

While we often cannot control our situations, we can control our responses to them.

I believe the saying is,

"We can become better or we can become bitter."

How we react to circumstances is a choice – and we often forget that and instead blame our foul mood, lack of sleep, or shortness with others on the circumstances of situations rather than recognizing the state of own heart.

Referring back to the text, during this time there was a barley harvest in Bethlehem – which means it was Spring as well as the beginning of a new season.

The Jewish people had recently celebrated the Passover/Feast of Unleavened Bread and were into the First Fruits celebration.

Christ is the fulfillment of the Passover (shedding of blood), a representation of the Unleavened Bread (sinless man), and the First Fruits (Jesus being the first fruit of the resurrection).

The life of embracing and practicing radical faith is a series of new beginnings.

Whatever heartache, sin, shame, or bitter times that you have had in the past or may be experiencing at this very moment – Jesus is waiting with open arms, patient and ready to be your new beginning.

Are you trusting God for this season in your life?

NOTES

The Beautiful & The Damned

For most of my childhood I felt like a misfit and I was terrified because nothing was definite or absolute at this point in our lives.

Everything was shifting.

We spent most of our childhood living out of motel rooms while my mother ran around the country escaping the police.

After she crashed the minivan, she was detained and we watched as they wrestled her into the back of the police car.

While my mother was in prison, my father sent us off to live with our grandparents in St. Tammany.

When she returned, learning to live as a family again, or seemingly for the first time, was awkward in the simplest of words.

For years prior we only ever heard our mothers voice recorded on cassette tapes as she recorded herself reading books to us.

When I first saw her walk through the door, I asked her a million times if it was truly her.

And when she spoke, I was frightened.

The voice had an unrecognizable face.

The woman that taught me to be radical and had exposed me to the virtue of willpower with the guidance of her voice was seemingly a foreigner.

By the age of eleven my older brother taught me how to clean my great grandmother's dialysis tubing, my twin sister taught me how to play blackjack, and I learned everything about my father during that period.

Even the grooves of his boot.

My friends and family members thought that I was matured at an early age.

But, honestly, I was just aware.

I would watch in agony as the pressure built up inside of people I loved.

Especially my father as he began to grow outwardly angry because of internal warfare.

Not abusively.

Just explosively.

I grew weary and frightened because I knew something was wrong, but every time I just tried to help or say something I would be smacked or banished.

Until I gained a new perspective accompanied by a deeper understanding of my father.

When my father had his first heart attack, his five sisters sat in the hospital with us telling the stories of my fathers' youth.

Willingly indulging the tales of the infamous and infallible Octavius Stone Jr.

Before he could walk, my father was working on his family farm outside of Cushing, Oklahoma.

On his eleventh birthday he witnessed his father suffer a massive heart attack as he sat in the passenger seat and veered into oncoming traffic before striking another car and rolling into an open field.

I only ever had the courage to ask my father once about the truthfulness behind the stories after he came home from the hospital.

He confided that he was forced to tear the rusted braces from each tooth with a pair of pliers because he could not go to the dentist after they lost their fathers health insurance.

He continued to grin showing us the divots in his teeth.

Any time after that he would say,

"Trust me, you don't even want to know," or,

"I didn't want you to be around her," regarding his mother as if she had a disease or a contagious infection that could potentially make me sick.

A few years later, my father told me the story about how he met my mother.

Shortly after his father's death, his mother and six sisters moved to New York and my father was sent to live with Uncle Merlin, Aunt Alma and their son,

Bertram, in Louisiana.

Four months later Aunt Alma passed away after suffering a massive stroke.

Less than a month later my father was arriving home from school with his cousin Bertram when they walked in and found that Uncle Merlin had committed suicide by putting a gun to his head and blowing his brains out all over his bedroom wall.

That is when my father was sent to Hope Haven in 1983 where he met my mother, Melody.

Neither were adopted before they reached the age of adulthood, and they decided to never leave each-others side.

But of all the things that I had learned about my father, nobody could explain anything about my mother.

New scars on top of old scars made us create stories rather than ask her to reveal them.

Even when I was just a child, I had become so consumed in figuring everything out that it completely wiped the childhood smile away from my face as I searched for answers instead of playing with my toys.

Something about knowing that they were able to make it through all of that, even as I could barely understand it, reassured my faith even when I could not define it.

So, as we sat at the table and I was eating my

microwaved pizza, I began to talk with her.

My mother did all she ever could possibly manage to take care of us, and that is the epitome of a resilience factor that she had never experienced in her own life before.

Her mother passed away during childbirth and her binger bound father was employed as a mafia member.

Her father, Alistair Ashmore, was inevitably lost in a perilous perspective of a time consumed with disheveled opportunities.

I like to remind myself that this is a time where most politicians were drug addicts, the majority of police and correctional officers were drug dealers, and truck drivers were allowed to drink on the job.

By the time my mother was fourteen years old, Alistair was growing exceedingly ill and undergoing chemotherapy treatments to battle his diagnosis of stage four lung and throat cancer.

The ironic clarity that came with sickness and the prognosis of inevitable death incited my grandfathers will to help others as he opened a church just before his passing.

Meanwhile my mother was then brought to Hope Haven.

My mother was orphaned, and my father was abandoned.

By some grace they met.

The reason I needed to understand that wasn't relevant to that moment, but it was relevant every single day after my mom returned with a disability that rendered her unable to work, and instead built businesses and grew into success after years of not being able to provide for us.

My father also taught me the only lesson I will ever need to keep in my heart and that is to stand rooted in love through all things.

Beautiful and blessed is the passion that drove me to pursue my purpose.

But damned and cursed is the everlasting love that could bind my spirit.

"Children inherit the qualities of the parents, no less than their physical features. Environment does play an important part, but the original capital on which a child starts in life is inherited from its ancestors. I have also seen children successfully surmounting the effects of an evil inheritance. That is due to purity being an inherent attribute of the soul."

-Mahatma Ghandi

Souvenirs Malléables

Over time it has faded from, into a vivid blur.

I knew something was hidden that I truly did not want to remember.

Bringing me into those years of captivity.

But what brought me out is something that I never want to forget.

Bringing me out of my comfortable yet traumatic zone.

The radical shift that put me into a blissful shock.

I cry out sometimes because I feel it has faded.

Still entranced in past experiences while pursuing the hopes of my future.

The worms on Reggie's grave still glistening with a faint silver.

The frost killed the crop that day.

The vegetables were soggy and tantalizing.

Yet pungent like Clifford's infected socks.

Anointed

He turns our weaknesses into his opportunities.

How, you may ask?

As we see the task ahead of us, I was reminded of these verses in **2 Corinthians**:

"Therefore, in order to keep me from becoming conceited, I was given a thorn in my flesh, a messenger of Satan, to torment me. Three times I pleaded with the Lord to take it away from me. But He said to me, "My grace is sufficient for you, for my power is made perfect in weakness." Therefore, I will boast all the more gladly about my weaknesses, so that Christ's power may rest on me. That is why, for Christ's sake, I delight in weaknesses, in insults, in hardships, in persecutions, in difficulties. For when I am weak, then I am strong."

We are the witnesses and ministers of the glory of God in this community.

As we are faced with circumstances and challenges, our weaknesses will be turned into His opportunities.

Do I have to remind you of what we have already experienced when we face such challenges?

God is Good.

We have a track record of seeing Him work efficaciously.

Our weakness is a proven opportunity.

"The harvest is plentiful, but the laborers are few; therefore, beseech the Lord of the harvest to send out laborers into His harvest." <u>Luke 10:2</u>

The job will always be bigger than our resources.

But we wake up every day and continue to work tirelessly as we are strengthened while serving His purposes.

"For God did not send His Son into the world to condemn the world, but to save the world through Him. Whoever believes in Him is not condemned, but whoever does not believe stands condemned already because they have not believed in the name of God's one and only Son. This is the verdict: Light has come into the world, but people loved darkness instead of light because their deeds were evil. Everyone who does evil hates the light and will not come into the light for fear that their deeds will be exposed." <u>John 3:17-20</u>

Jesus came to bring salvation.

But these verses also epitomize the fact that even though He came to bring salvation, there are still many who will reject His word.

We cannot control everything, nor will we be accepted everywhere, nor by everybody - but we can be faithful and obedient to the Lord who calls us to reach out into our community with unconditional love.

So, knowing the challenges and our calling, what shall we do?

"Now may the God of peace, who through the blood of the eternal covenant brought back from the dead our Lord Jesus, that great Shepherd of the sheep, equip you with everything good for doing His will, and may he work in us what is pleasing to Him, through Jesus Christ, to whom be glory for ever and ever. Amen." <u>Hebrews 13:20</u>

God equips us with everything good for doing His will.

We should be prepared and ready to face our challenges and trust that He will bring us through.

The first thing we want to explore in the future is the question of identity.

We have often asked the question of who are we in God?

But who are we in our intentions?

We used to intend to do God's will - but today, many intend to hurt rather than heal.

When we truly come to God our intentions begin to reflect our relationship with Him.

What do we stand for?

What can we contribute?

What are our strengths and weaknesses?

What sells us?

What has God made special about us that will make a difference to others?

When we can answer that quandary, we can begin to equip ourselves better in unification to fulfill God's purposes.

<u>NOTES</u>

Raspberry Jammed

The raspberries were even more delicious as the sun warmed them up.

My great-grandmother had a bunch of raspberry bushes in the backyard about 4 yards away from the vegetable garden that my brother, Octavius III, my sister, Ophelia, and I would fill buckets and bags to the brim for her to make homemade jam with.

Well, with the rest of the raspberries we did not either spill or eat on the way back inside.

Truly we were never supposed to be in that garden.

The graceful woman who let three rowdy kids roll around and tear away at her raspberry bushes was a blessing we inherited before we ever stepped foot in a church.

That graceful woman, being my great grandmother by love Ms. Mabel Wakefield, had the most invigorating angelic effervescence that emitted much more intensely than any other person I have ever been in the presence of in my entire life.

My ancestors and relatives, most being rambunctious and some merely erroneous at heart, predisposed certain aspects of my personality to view any form of nurturing or positivity as a burden.

I inherited a weak temper, a vile vocabulary, and a depressingly skewed perception.

I fought to withstand the temptation of my own genetic disposition.

However, I instead turned my inherited anger into discouragement and self-hatred.

All I ever knew was how to hate myself, my thoughts, and the things that I do while I love others despite their infidelities and wickedness.

Yet, she was always gentle, generous, and vivacious, with a grace in her hands that would cradle your soul for eternity if you let it.

She was the one person I can truly recall that touched my heart and changed my life by walking in grace.

Her spirit drove me at an early age, stricken and strewn with circumstances and by temptations plentiful.

I was bound to nurture even if it was not my nature.

Watching Mabel go blind and identify us by hearing our voices was my first breaking point.

I would have never understood the premise of a catalyst lest I encountered a myriad throughout my young adult life.

One of my earliest being the time when I was twelve years old and Clifford put me to work on his butcher farm slaughtering pigs and shoveling swine dung.

Whenever my grandfather left to distribute the haul in town, my cousin Gideon would lock Ophelia and Octavius III in their bedrooms.

Then, Gideon would spar with me in the basement, often knocking me unconscious and then locking me in for hours.

One day I decided to finally break off the door handle and Gideon proceeded to drag me by a handful of hair out to the bayou.

He stuffed filthy, bloody slabs of raw pork into my pockets and then he threw me into the water, repeatedly striking my face and kicking my hands off the side of the shallow shore as I tried to climb back out of the water, leaving my face swollen and my fingers blistered and crooked.

When Clifford returned and saw me sitting there wounded in the corner crawled up into a blood-soaked ball, he literally beat Gideon half to death before sending him off to a boarding school in Pennsylvania.

Things back home really could not bother me after that.

The humiliation of being followed home from school and smacked with shards of blacktop and garbage while bullies screamed and scrutinized the emblems on my clothes could not even compare.

Yet, I was further exposed to insolent reality as the kids who sat beside me in school were stuffing dime bags in their boxer briefs and trying to sell it to other school kids.

A mother sold her infant daughter for drug money just around the corner from where I grew up.

Innocent children were yoked up and sometimes shot on the same street I used to foolishly walk every day.

It seemed that no matter where I looked, I could only find the impurities and injustices as I sought for the healing my heart desired.

My luck diminished when I was fifteen years old weighing over three-hundred-pounds and standing above six-foot as I naturally became a labeled target for the older folk around the way.

A thousand times my father would say,

"Don't go down on Second Ave," just before we left the house to go run the streets.

Every time we either got stopped and patted down by the police or heckled and even spat at by the local bando dwellers.

One time we were approached by a belligerent man who was likely high on drugs that began to scream incoherently and repeatedly so all would turn and watch him punch and scrape his hands across the sidewalk until his hands were bloodied.

Our friend, Jasper, rushed down the street hauling a hatchet and chased the deranged man through traffic before both were arrested.

We were standing directly in front of the apartment where my Uncle Eldridge was murdered.

A few months later my best friend, Silas Sterling, and I stopped at the local pizza shop after football practice and met up with our two friends from school, Ruth Wraith and Esther Sinnet.

Ruth had offered to buy us food and asked us to walk home with them afterwards since we lived on the same block.

On our way home, we decided to walk through the alley to get to the only store that would casually sell tobacco products to fourteen and fifteen-year-old kids, which incidentally was on Second Ave.

On our way through the alley just a block before the store, we were ambushed, battered, and robbed by three masked men across from the same street I foolishly walked home every day.

What scared me the most was the way the girls looked back at me as I could only feel the gun pressed up against the back of my head, but they could see it.

I glanced over at the men beating Silas over the head with a rock and looked back over at the girls huddled in the corner and instinctively yelled,

"Run!"

One thought went through my mind.

Fight.

Frozen in anxiety, I was unsure of whether I was going to walk away alive and contemplating what happens after the gun goes off.

Silas was still getting smacked in the face and kicked in his torso while he laid there unconscious.

The two attackers left him lying face down in the dirt as they turned and approached me yelling,

"WHERE THE MONEY AT!"

Almost instinctively I cheekily replied,

"What money?"

I then remember being swarmed and barraged with blows to the head and body until I collapsed to the ground enveloped in dull pain.

I would have been able to count a cadence of the strikes if the noise of broken ribs rubbing together did not drown out the bludgeoning.

I closed my eyes and prayed that it was over.

For a moment I did not feel anything.

I could no longer hear the crunching of my glasses in the snow anymore.

I couldn't hear anything.

I never woke up; I just felt my lungs take in air again.

In the same instance of drooling a waterfall of blood from my mouth to the ground and pulling myself to face Silas, I watched as a straggling attacker ran back to deliver a final blow to my friend.

Without a thought I knocked the shadow against the chain link fence with my shoulder and punched the figure in the face until my hand shattered.

Then, I heard the gun go off behind me.

I didn't even look back before I aimlessly took a grasp of Silas' clothing and dragged him until I felt pins and needles rush up my spine.

Every step took everything I had.

Within a breath I was staring Silas in his unconscious eyes.

Within a heartbeat I was waking up in the hospital.

Not only did I go home every night and torture myself over what I looked like and what people would say about me, but I was now faced with an infirmity that held me back from proving them wrong.

At some point thereafter, I remember thinking to myself,

"I wish they just ended it right there."

Had I only known they were almost successful as the affluent knife wounds were merely inches away from lacerating my thoracic aorta, and the bullet wound just missed my spinal cord.

For the years to come that I would have to fear over the possibilities of what almost happened yesterday.

Sometimes, I think the pain that comes along with reliving the anxiety of almost being murdered is just as excruciating as enduring it.

That someone, or more than one, would be willing to take my life with his or her own hands.

Or with the eight-inch steak knife that was recovered

next to my best friends' bloodied body and my broken glasses.

The brain damage only instigated the migraines I was predisposed to through years of consuming anti-depressant medications.

The physical wounds healed gracefully.

But the real wound was hidden.

The one that never healed.

The one that had started growing the first time I got cut.

The one that stretched and peeled away the flesh of my spirit over time.

My friends never knew that it was not possible for me to 'love' like them.

Without having ever loved at all.

Although, I admit, I truly do not know all there is to know about this thing called 'love'.

While other young boys were playing video games and running for touchdowns, I held my sister Ophelia and wept with her as she relived the horror of her past.

It didn't take long for me to associate the defilement of my loved ones with the devious acts of carnality acted out by men and women alike.

Though personally considered psychotic and manipulative, I believe that any sex before knowledge of the concept of what marriage truly is, is unclean.

Each of you should know the roles you play in life.

As well as in each other's life.

As I watched lives unravel before my own eyes because of the pursuit of immediate gratification, it destroyed a piece of me.

It destroyed the peace in me.

I was in a dark place.

Asphyxiating with a marijuana filled cigar.

Chain smoking like the people I cried over inhaled the second-hand smoke.

Like they were there with me, but I was alone.

It was only hard to breathe when I was thinking.

I told everyone I was right here, but I never actually said it to them.

I was never there.

For some time, I would swat cameras and deny taking any photos, let alone look at myself in the mirror.

I would lock myself away and cry until it felt as if my eye lids were being scraped against sandpaper.

When I returned to school in hopes to be received in open arms, the intensity of my hot flashes and anxiety ended up skyrocketing as I sat in class with wounds that nobody could see.

It wasn't a cast all my friends could sign or a crutch that aided in dispersing of a crowd from your personal space.

The fluorescent lights instigated my migraines and the bantering in the hallways further provoked the excruciating ringing from the top of my skull to the bottom of my neck.

I was broken on the outside and hemorrhaging on the inside.

Hemorrhaging for the lack of support.

Friends.

Money.

Love.

I was even hemorrhaging for my family.

As they were hurting, and I had to watch them fall deeper into the abyss.

I was thinking to myself,

"I can't pull them out, I don't believe I am not strong enough."

But then I was reminded,

"I can do all things through Christ who strengthens me."

Philippians 4:13

And then I spoke.

Once I had the power to utter the words locked away

in my heart, I unconsciously made the commitment to never look back and chose to fight for everything righteous while I put pressure on my open wounds.

The words I spoke brought healing not only for myself, but for the people watching me smile in public and accrue massive success in certain areas and then go home to deal with my own personal afflictions.

They came to realize how worried I was and they more than related to it.

They never knew I was so scared, until I said something.

Somewhere in the back of my head, I always had a vision that the purpose of everything that I worked on and sweated over that was only purposed to unite and empower others.

And everything that I would divulge and admit to would be for the same reason.

It was never for me.

I didn't even know why or what I was doing, but I knew I was called to it.

To put others before myself.

I was still confused over the fact that if I could explain my circumstances with such proclivity and relate to people in the process then how can I understand it, know exactly how to fix it and still not know where to go?

The problem was that I was too busy trying to create

a purpose that I didn't recognize it while I was holding onto it and I almost abandoned it because I had no idea that it belonged to me.

As time passed by, I missed many opportunities and grew to become severely depressed and extremely overweight.

I fought many times to counter the opposition and the enemies against me, but I could never get through the battle in my own head.

As I fought to become 'normal' I was beaten, bruised, broken, and injured.

One morning while recovering after one of many surgeries I remember sitting in my room staring at the abundance of medications stretched across my dresser.

I hated the way they made me feel.

That day I took them as usual and everything seemed ordinary.

Then, as I was sitting in the living room I felt as if my chest was caving in, then my ears began to ring, and my eyes were blinded even as I held them open with my fingers.

I woke up at the kitchen table to a bowl of microwave noodles and my family surrounding me.

I flushed everything down the toilet and told my doctor I was never taking any medication ever again, suffering the rest of my recovery in agonizing pain.

I was allowed to recover.

But I wasn't allowed to get into what I got out for.

The doctors told me I couldn't, shouldn't and probably wouldn't.

I was obligated to believe otherwise.

I remember going home and asking my father if he could purchase a gym membership, but we didn't have that kind of money.

So, he did the best he could do.

My first gym was a shady shack with collapsed ceilings and corroded key locks hidden in the back yard of a residence soon to be condemned that belonged to my father's friend.

I would either wrap t-shirts around my head in the winter or move the weights out in the middle of the alley during the summer, so I didn't get Mesothelioma.

Each strike upon the punching bag knocked the asbestos residue over the makeshift bench press and the rusted plates slopped in the corner that strictly kept the cardboard wall in place.

The viciously mold-ridden walls would bend and crumble with the wind releasing the eighty unusual species of spiders embedded within the cardboard.

Several oddly placed and tattered tarps covered all the holes in the roof and would fill with stagnant water, frozen squirrels, and rotten birds.

For years I would take that walk from my house with two forty-five-pound plates to the shifty shed five blocks away from my house through the alleys of Lansingburgh in the middle of darkness because I couldn't stand the light.

I would have rather been tortured alive then to endure another migraine.

The deviated knuckles, abundance of calluses, bent fingers, crooked jaw and all my beautiful scars will tell the pain I put myself through just to change what people said about me, and my success in the end changed what I said about myself.

I do deserve to be loved.

"Character is always known. Thefts never enrich, Alms never impoverish, Murder will speak out of stone walls."

-Ralph Waldo Emerson

"Darkness cannot drive out darkness; Only light can do that. Hate cannot drive out hate; Only love can do that."

-Martin Luther King Jr.

Interlude I

I have stood on the decks of aircraft carriers, naval destroyers and amphibious vessels as men and women serving our nation prepared to go into battle.

I have watched as uplifted faces with earnest expressions seem to be saying to me,

"Chaplain, what if I am not alive when the sun sets on tomorrow? What can you tell me that will make a difference?"

I have visited families to inform them that their loved one perished in combat.

And many of these people cry out to God.

Yet, He answers them not a word.

And they, along with many of us, have the challenge of trying to learn how to deal with the silence of God.

In the scriptures, we encounter a Canaanite woman who had to deal with the silence of God.

<u>Matthew 15</u>, beginning with verse 21:

"Leaving that place, Jesus withdrew to the region of Tyre and Sidon. A Canaanite woman from that vicinity came to Him, crying out, 'Lord, son of David, have mercy on me. My daughter is suffering terribly from demon possession.' And He answered her not a word."

When I was growing up, I was about nine or ten

years of age and I overheard my mother talking about one of the deacons in the church.

She said,

"He makes big money."

And I kept my antenna up so that I could hear what the figure was, and eventually she said,

"He makes $400 a week."

I went to my bedroom; it was time to go to sleep and I did not pray my usual prayer.

I prayed a sincere prayer,

"Lord, if you will grant this request, I will never ask you for anything else for as long as I live. If you will let me one day grow up and make $100 a week, you will never hear another petition from my lips."

Are you not as glad as I that God does not always say,

"Yes" to our prayers?

If He had done so, it is probable that I would likely not be able to fill up my gas tank today.

He had locked a door that I prayed to open and kept me out of that $100 a week that I prayed for.

Similarly, years later I was in college and I met a young woman.

We had Microbiology class together and for some reason when I saw her, the words of Christopher Marlowe's 'Faustus' leapt to mind,

74

"Is this the face that launched a thousand ships? O Helen, by thy beauty I am enthralled. Thou art fairer than the evening air clad in the beauty of a thousand stars."

I went back to my room and fell on my knees.

And since I had not yet been granted the previous petition, I prayed,

"Lord, God of the universe, if you will grant this request, I will never ask you for anything else for as long as I live. I saw a damsel today. I felt something beautiful in my heart and if somehow you can let her feel what I feel, so that together, we will traverse the seasons, I will never ask you for anything else for as long as I live."

Well God said,

"No."

And when I met the woman I would later marry I said,

"Thank you, Lord! Thank you! Thank you! Thank you!"

I no longer mind when God either says,

"No," or nothing at all - because I trust His omniscience.

He is all wise.

Nevertheless, when He says nothing, we still go through what Scott Fitzgerald called,

"The dark night of the soul."

It is a place of uncertainty and confusion that usually leads to something better than you had in mind before.

Even more concerning is understanding the fact that sometimes He says nothing because of our sins and transgressions.

Which so many times leads us to attribute His silence to our disobedience.

Isaiah 59:1-2 says,

"The Lord's arm is not short that He cannot reach you - His ears are not heavy that He cannot hear. Your iniquities have come between you and God."

Like Saul, in **1 Samuel 28**, seeking answers from a Witch of Endor because of the silence of God.

Sometimes He is also silent because we are not ready to hear what He has to reveal.

In **John 16:12** (Jesus is speaking to His disciples in His farewell discourse), He said,

"There are many things I want to tell you, but you are not ready to hear them yet."

Sometimes God is silent because we do not have the proper motives or intentions.

James 4:3 says,

"You ask and you don't receive because you ask amiss that you might spend it on your own pleasures."

Sometimes, God is silent because of our lack of faith.

Much like the disciples in **Matthew 17** who unsuccessfully attempted to cast out a demon.

And they failed.

Later, they came to Jesus and said,

"Why was God silent? What happened?"

And Jesus said,

"It was because of your lack of faith. It was because of your unbelief."

I am so glad that the Canaanite woman had such a prepossessing faith as illustrated in **Matthew 15:21-28**.

Our Blessed Lord says,

"Woman, you have great faith. Your request is granted."

And her daughter was healed that very hour.

This woman teaches us how to deal with the silence of God.

How do you deal with it yourself?

I suggest you should let love be your motivation.

Many times, God is silent because of the selfish nature of our prayers.

This woman comes to Jesus not to get something for herself, but to get something for her daughter.

If you are going to deal with the silence of God, let love be your motivation.

But also, if you are going to deal with His silence, know that He is present and listening even when He does not speak.

David said in the **139th Psalm,**

"How can I flee from your spirit? If I ascend into heaven, you are there. If I make my bed in hell, you are there. If I take the wings of the morning and dwell in the uttermost parts of the sea, even there, your right hand will uphold me."

God is listening, even when He doesn't speak.

Do you recall the story of Mary and Martha?

Lazarus is sick in **John 11**.

Jesus is not in Bethany where they live, and so they send word to Jesus by a messenger:

"The one whom you love is sick."

They know that Jesus will know what to do.

In **John 11:4**, Jesus says to the messenger,

"This sickness is not unto death, but for the glory of God."

And the messenger scurries away with the great news to Mary and Martha.

As Lazarus' condition deteriorates, there is no doubt that they are perplexed.

And they probably greeted the news of Lazarus' death with incredulity.

"It can't be. The Master said Lazarus is not going to die."

And where is Jesus now?

He is silent.

He answers them not a word.

"Surely, He will be at the funeral."

He is not there.

He says absolutely nothing.

Although, He had a plan in store for Lazarus.

He is indeed listening even when He doesn't speak.

He shows up after Lazarus has been dead for days.

You can imagine, Mary and Martha have a little bit of an attitude and some resentment towards Jesus.

Mary doesn't even go out to greet Jesus.

Martha does.

And she comes out with amazing words.

She says to Jesus - not as a chastisement but as affirmation:

"Lord, if you had been here, my brother would not have died."

But then she continues,

"But I know that even now, anything you ask of God, He will give it to you."

79

The silence would soon be broken as our Blessed Lord stands at the sepulcher and speaks three simple words:

"Lazarus, come forth."

The words roll from His lips and float along the ethereal waves into the darkened sepulcher, and commingled with inanimate clay, and life springs anew in the breast of a dead man because the Lord of Life simply said,

"Get up."

He had been silent, but now He is speaking in His undeniably omnipotent way.

Know that He is listening even when he doesn't speak.

He said to Moses after 400 years,

"I've heard them. I have seen what their oppressors have done. Go down into Egypt and tell Pharaoh to let my people go."

When God says nothing, let love be your motivation.

The **First Psalm** says,

"Blessed is the man that walks not in the counsel of the ungodly, nor stands in the way of sinners, nor sits in the seat of the scornful, but his delight is in the law of the Lord, the word of God. And in that law, he meditates day and night."

How often during the week do you meditate on Scripture?

There are answers in God's word.

"In the beginning was the Word, and the Word was with God, and the Word was God. The same was in the beginning with God. All things were made by Him, and without Him was not anything made that was made."

We find His voice in the Word.

The Psalms are overwhelmingly powerful.

Every human emotion is captured by the Psalms.

The Gospels are illuminating.

Four biographies of our Blessed Lord.

The reality is, my brothers and sisters:

Jesus is in every part of the Word.

He said in **John 5:39**,

"Search the Scriptures; for in them, you think you have eternal life, and these are they which testify of me."

In **Genesis**, He is, *"Shiloh."*

In **Exodus**, He is the, *"I Am."*

In **Numbers**, He is the, *"Star and Scepter."*

In **Deuteronomy**, He is the, *"Rock."*

In Joshua, He is, *"Captain of the Lord's host."*

In Psalms, He is the, *"Great Shepherd."*

In Proverbs, He is the, *"Beloved."*

Isaiah called Him, *"Wonderful Counselor,"* as well as *"The Mighty God, the Everlasting Father, the Prince of Peace."*

Micah said, *"He is the one whose going forth of old is from everlasting to everlasting."*

Zachariah called Him the, *"Branch."*

Malachi called Him the, *"Messenger of the Covenant."*

Matthew said, *"Savior."*

Mark said, *"Son of Man."*

Luke said, *"The Great Physician."*

John said, *"The Word made flesh."*

Acts said, *"He is the one who empowers you to witness."*

Philippians said, *"He is the name above every name and one day at the name of Jesus, every knee will bow, and every tongue confess that he is Lord to the glory of God, the Father."*

Thessalonians said, *"He is the One who will descend from heaven with a shout, with the voice of the archangel and the trump of God, and the dead in Christ shall rise."*

Hebrews said, *"He's the great High Priest, touched with the feelings of our infirmities, in all points tempted like us, yet without sin."*

Jude said, *"He is able to keep you without stumbling or slipping and to present you without fault or blemish before the presence of His glory with unspeakable ecstatic delight in triumphant joy and exaltation."*

In Revelation, John, a prisoner on the Isle of Patmos in the Aegean Sea said,

"I was in the spirit on the Lord's day. I saw Him high and lifted up in my solitary place. He is Alpha, He is Omega, He is Beginning, He is Ending, He is Author, He is Finisher, He is King of kings and Lord of lords."

For some of you, this may be a time when you must again deal with the silence of God.

Keep the lines of communication open.

Let love be your motivation.

And what you will discover is:

"Weeping may endure for a night, but joy will come in the morning."

NOTES

Interlude II

There is a desperate need of healing in our world.

I grew up in the toxic pathology of a ghetto on the outskirts of Albany, New York.

My mother was in Prison and came to learn more about the Bible behind bars than most ever do sitting in pews.

She attempted to inoculate us against the pathology of our environment.

And she did very well - through action and consistency.

She insisted on the King James Version.

She said,

"If it was good enough for Jesus, it's good enough for you."

So, if you would go to my home, you would see a young me combing the Scriptures, not looking for spiritual nourishment, but for short verses.

I was assiduously pursuing the low-hanging fruit.

And to this very day, my favorite Bible verses are the short ones.

<u>John 11:35</u>:

"Jesus wept."

<u>Luke 17:32:</u>

"Remember Lot's wife."

<u>1 Thessalonians 5</u> is a treasure trove; verse 16 says:

"Rejoice evermore."

Verse 17: *"Pray without ceasing."*

Verse 18: *"Don't quench the spirit."*

The Word of God brought emotional healing to me.

It gave me a defense shield against anything that would try to eviscerate my self-esteem.

I was only ten years of age and I read:

"For we are not redeemed by corruptible things such as silver and gold, but with the precious blood of Jesus, as a lamb without spot or blemish."

And to my pre-pubescent mind came the insight that the value of an object is based upon the price someone is willing to pay.

And I comprehended the fact that God sent His Son to give His life for me.

It infused me with such a spirit of somebody-ness that nothing that happened to me after that could change my sense that the image of God had been stamped on me - that I was of inestimable value.

That is the healing power of the Word of God.

In order to experience the healing power of the Word of God, we must pay the cost for the cure.

In **Luke 4**, Jesus was in His hometown and He stood up and read from Isaiah:

"The spirit of the Lord God is upon me because He has anointed me to preach good news to the poor. He has sent me to bring deliverance to captives, the recovery of sight to the blind, to set at liberty those who are bruised."

He came on a mission of healing and He said in **John 20:21**:

"As the Father has sent me, I am sending you."

He left the chants of cherubim and the songs of seraphim.

He left unpolluted breezes and un-darkened days.

He left the Father's presence and a rainbow-encircled throne in a land where night never comes.

To have a breakthrough at Bethlehem.

To bring healing to our world.

And He says to you and me:

"I send you to do the same thing, to bring healing to our world."

In the story of the judgment in **Matthew 25**, God is not interested in theological orthodoxy.

The 'Judge of the Universe' does not make the query,

"Did you sprinkle or immerse?"

Or,

"Do you believe in transubstantiation or consubstantiation?"

None of that.

Instead, He asks six pointed questions, each dealing with healing in our world:

Did you feed the hungry?

Did you give water to the thirsty?

Did you clothe the naked?

Did you visit the sick?

Did you minister to the incarcerated?

Did you take care of the strangers?

Our blessed Lord gave us principles to bring healing to our world and He wants us to be His agents of healing, continuing His messianic thrust of setting the captives free.

The fact of the matter is that most of us that are unwilling to pay the cost for the cure.

You want healing in your intellectual development?

David said in **Psalm 119:99**:

"I have more wisdom than all of my teachers because I meditate upon your Word."

Do you want healing in terms of your spiritual growth and development?

<u>Proverbs 1:7</u> says:

"The fear of the Lord [reverential awe] is the beginning of wisdom. "

Do you want healing in terms of your physical well-being?

<u>1 Corinthians 9:27</u> says:

"I keep my body under control and make it my slave, lest after I have preached to others, I myself will be disqualified."

Do you want national healing?

<u>2 Chronicles 7:14</u> says:

"If my people called by my name will humble themselves and pray and seek my face and turn from their wicked ways. Then will I hear from heaven, forgive their sins and heal their land."

In **Genesis 18**, as Abraham negotiated for the survival of Sodom and Gomorrah, he said,

"Lord if there are ten righteous people left in those cities will you spare the cities?"

In **Matthew 5**, we read:

"You are the salt of the earth."

Before refrigeration and salt preserves, we meet a woman who needs healing.

And there is a price for her cure.

For twelve years she had spent her money on

physicians without any improvement.

The Talmud had eleven cures for hemorrhaging, and I am sure she tried all of those; many of them had nothing to do with good medicine and more with superstition.

One was,

"Get the ashes of an ostrich, place it in a lemon napkin in the summer time and a wool napkin in the winter time, and carry that around with you and you will be cured of your issue of blood."

She tried it all - and like so many of us, she came to Jesus as her last resort.

And yet, I am happy to tell you, the good news is - even if Jesus is your last chance, He is still your best chance.

We find that this woman could not go into the synagogue because she was ceremonially unclean.

She was cut off from the homilies of the rabbis.

But she started talking to herself, and she said,

"If I can only touch the hem of His garment... I will be made whole."

There are actually two stories of healing occurring in this Bible passage.

Immediately before this woman's encounter with Jesus, a ruler of the synagogue named Jairus came to Him and said:

"Jesus, my daughter is dying. Will you come to my

home and heal her?"

And Jesus said,

"Let's go."

So, they started walking.

And suddenly - Jesus stops and says,

"Somebody touched me."

I believe it was Peter who, in essence, said,

"Lord, what are you talking about - somebody's touching you? Everybody is always reaching out at you, wants your autograph. What do you mean somebody's touching you?"

Jesus said,

"No, no, no, this was different. Power went out of me. Virtue went out of me."

There was a cost for this cure.

"Who touched me?"

And the Bible says she told all.

That was a long testimony - she told it from start to finish.

"Twelve years ago, it started happening. I went to Dr. Smith. I went to Dr. Combs. I went to so-and-so."

On and on it went.

And through the words of her testimony she received healing.

She paid the cost for the cure through her testimony.

There are a few principles present that guide us towards paying the cost for our own cure.

    1.) Give of your substance and strength to bring healing.

The Bible says in **Luke 6**:

"Give and it shall be given unto you."

Galatians 6:2 says:

"Bear ye one another's burdens and so fulfill the law of Christ."

We have got to give of our substance and our strength.

A wonderful parable of the Good Samaritan in **Luke 10**, a man wounded on the highway desperately needed healing.

Priests came by - he is ceremonially unclean.

They cannot touch him.

A Levite came – and went.

Then, out of nowhere appears a Gentile (a Samaritan) who comes and gives his substance and his strength.

He dresses the wounds.

He pours the oil.

He provides transportation to shelter.

Then, as he is departing, he turns around and says,

"If there are additional expenses, go ahead and slap it on my tab."

Are you willing to give of your substance and your strength?

I think of Gandhi - born in Bombay, educated as a barrister in England.

He travelled to South Africa and was thrown off of a train.

It so transformed him that he gave up his substance and his strength to bring healing to his beloved India.

And who would have guessed at the time when he was assassinated in 1948, that the seeds he planted for healing would inspire a young African American drum major for justice, truth, and righteousness - Martin Luther King Jr.

Give of your substance and give of your strength to bring healing.

2.) Exercise majestic faith.

<u>Hebrews 11:6</u> says:

"Without faith it is impossible to please God."

Faith is the only spiritual attribute that scripture says without it, it is impossible to please God.

If you want to please God, exercise faith - and the greater the faith, the more you please Him.

Our blessed Lord encountered the centurion in

<u>Matthew 8</u>.

The centurion came to Him and said,

"My servant is dying could you please come. My servant is dying would you please heal him?"

And Jesus said,

"Let's go."

The centurion, a military man, said,

"You don't have to go to my house Jesus. I am a man under authority. I say 'Jump' and the troops say: 'How high, sir?' Speak the word and my servant will be healed."

Now, only twice in the New Testament is this particular Greek verb - that Jesus was 'amazed'.

It is difficult to amaze Jesus.

The Bible says Jesus was amazed by this Gentile soldier.

In essence, Jesus said,

"Who are you? How could you possibly know that I can heal long-distance?"

The only other time the Greek verb for 'amazed' is used is in **Mark 6**, verses 5 and 6, where Jesus goes home, and His hometown people reject Him:

"Is not this the carpenter's son?"

And the Bible says in **Mark 6:5**:

"He could not do many mighty works there because

of their unbelief."

Are we missing blessings because of our failure to exercise majestic faith?

George Bernard Shaw said,

"Some people see things that are and ask: Why? I dream things that never were and ask, Why not?"

Jack Kennedy in May of 1961 says:

"We're going to put a man on the moon by the end of the decade and bring him back safely to earth.'"

And when most of the world heard that, I put my top dollar on the fact that many thought he was he was going insane.

But it happened!

If the exercise of faith in the secular realm can achieve the ostensibly impossible, think of what will happen if we pay the cost for the cure and exercise majestic faith!

It took majestic faith for this woman to say:

"If I can reach out and touch the hem of His garment, I will be made whole."

3.) Persevere through the obstacles.

Inevitably, when you are attempting to bring healing, there will be obstacles.

That is why **Galatians 6:9** tells us:

"Do not become weary in well doing, for in due

season you will reap if you faint not."

There will be obstacles.

In **Mark 2**, some friends bring a paralytic friend to Jesus.

They get to where Jesus is preaching.

The front door is closed, but as the philosopher J.R. Ewing said,

"If you can't get in the front door, go around to the back."

So, they went around to the back – but they couldn't get in that way either.

Then they went up to the roof and lowered this man at the feet of Jesus.

When Jesus saw their faith, He first gave the man spiritual healing because spiritual healing is often the prelude to physical healing.

He said to the paralytic:

"Your sins be forgiven."

Let us not major in minors.

Let us start with spiritual healing.

The power of our blessed Lord bringing healing to those who would persevere through the obstacle.

Imagine that diminutive woman drained through the years, weakened, pushing through that crowd, reaching out, and persevering.

Then finally reaching Jesus.

We must pay the cost for the cure.

And we must not get discouraged.

We shall overcome because the arc of the moral universe is young, and it bends toward justice.

We shall reap what we sew.

Persevere through the obstacles.

And finally:

4.) Bring healing with your testimony.

This woman is outed by Jesus.

As she tells her story, Jairus is listening and he remembers - my daughter is twelve years of age.

Somehow, his daughter and this woman are connected.

He places this woman's story of victorious healing into juxtaposition with his story of despair.

He needs a stronger foundation on which to base his faith.

While Jesus continues his conversation with this woman, Jairus' servant comes and says,

"Your daughter is dead. Why trouble the master any longer?"

And I believe it was that woman's testimony that gave Jairus enough faith to follow Jesus to his home anyhow.

Otherwise, if Jairus had listened to his servants doubts, Jesus would not have raised his daughter from the dead.

In this very chapter of **Mark 5**, Jesus also heals the demoniac of the Gerasene's.

This man nobody could contain.

Running among the tombs.

Breaking the chains fashioned to bind him.

And when Jesus sends demons into screeching pigs, this man says,

"Let me go with you Jesus. I do not want to stay here." And Jesus says: "No, we need your testimony."

Isn't that what **Revelation 12: 11** is talking about?

They overcame through the blood of the Lamb and through the words of their testimony.

They paid the cost for the cure.

All kinds of problems are in our world but give of your substance and your strength.

Exercise a majestic faith.

Matthew 17 says,

"If you've got faith the size of the grain of a mustard seed you can move mountains."

Persevere through the obstacles.

And let your testimony transform lives.

NOTES

Interlude III

Do you think it is still possible in the 21st century to speak about God in the public places when we celebrate or support our country?

I suggest that Abraham Lincoln can be our guide, and that after 140 years, his words are strangely and wonderfully timeless as we attempt to answer that question.

Lincoln's second inaugural address was delivered on March 4, 1865, before a crowd of 35,000 to 40,000 people.

They had come through terrible wind and rain that day to hear the President after this tumultuous war.

620,000 dead.

So, as I read the letters and diaries of those coming to the inauguration, I expected to find a mood of celebration, jubilation, and expectation - but I found something else.

In these letters, I found a mood of anger.

These persons present, almost every one of whom had lost a husband, brother, or a son, were deeply angry at the other side, the enemy, who had caused these deaths.

No doubt they would have cheered had Abraham Lincoln given voice to that anger in this second inaugural address.

People were just settling in as he was concluding, as it was only 6-7 minutes long.

In 701 words, Lincoln mentions God fourteen times, quotes scripture four times and invokes prayer three times.

This second inaugural address offers us, I believe, a guide for how you and I can answer the question:

"How do we speak about God in the public places of our lives?"

The first clue is Lincoln's use of what I call 'inclusive language'.

Rather than demonizing the South, he was already asking the question:

"How do we bring the South back into the Union?"

And he understood that if they alone were to bear the blame and the shame that they would never be brought back into the Union again.

So, notice at the beginning of the second paragraph Lincoln says:

"... on the occasion corresponding to this four years ago, all thoughts were anxiously directed to an impending civil war. All dreaded it. All sought to avert it."

Lincoln is giving the best intentions to the supposed enemy, the South, towards the end of the paragraph by insisting that BOTH parties deprecated war.

And we also will hear him say that both soldiers from

different sides read the same Bible.

In our multi-religious and multi-cultural world, as you and I wish to give witness to our faith in Jesus Christ, need to begin with respectful listening.

With giving our best intentions to others who are aspiring in their own way to discover some meaning of truth.

To offer respect and to listen.

This is Lincoln's posture and it sets the parameters for what he wishes to say.

But the real question is:

"How will we give resources to our witness.? How will we speak?"

As authorities in Gettysburg prepared for the dedication of a first national military cemetery and had invited Edward Everett and, secondly, Abraham Lincoln to speak - they had a monumental task before them.

They had 50,000 dead, wounded, or missing soldiers and they decided that they would take everything off the bodies of the soldiers- money, letters, diaries... anything that was theirs so it could be catalogued and families could come and collect it.

What they chiefly found were Bibles.

And you can find Lincoln say:

"... both read from the same Bible, and pray to the same God,"

He is signaling to us that he intends to think theologically as well as politically about the meaning of the Civil War.

His first words are words of affirmation.

I think of Lincoln as a C.S. Lewis, as you can read the Chronicles of Narnia and children and grandchildren, 6-7 year old's can grasp its meaning - but you can also as an adult or young adult, go back and read the Chronicles again and see the deep, deep truths that are embedded there.

After affirming in inclusive language that both read the same Bible and pray to the same God, he then puts the sticker into it as each invokes the aid of the other.

He had become very tired of the delegations of both politicians and ministers who came to him over and over again to say:

"God is on our side."

One day, he said:

"Don't you think if God is on our side that the President of the United States would become part of the conversation?"

And then one day he said:

"I'm not as concerned about whether or not God is on our side. I want to know how I can get on God's side."

Remember the expectations of the audience - they wanted Lincoln to judge the South.

Lincoln quickly disabuses that by invoking Jesus' Sermon on the Mount.

This particular sermon is rooted in humility and passion.

Truly blessed are those who do not follow the way of the world, the way of judgment and criticism.

Jesus' moral light comes through this Sermon on the Mount and this is the center of Lincoln's second inaugural address.

A lot of critics and cynics have said:

"Well, I wonder if this is just the shrewd language of a politician."

All of those people who were close to him gave multiple examples of evidence of his use of the Bible.

Rebecca Pomeroy was a nurse who was called into the White House after the death of Willie Lincoln.

Mary Lincoln was in a difficult state, so she was there to care for her.

As they would gather for lunch every day, Rebecca Pomeroy would notice that Abraham Lincoln would sit there in a rocking chair and take his shoes off, and she would quickly put his slippers on, and he would take out the old Bible and one day he said to her,

"What is your favorite portion of the Bible?"

And she said,

"Psalms."

And Lincoln said,

"Me, too. I've memorized a good portion of it."

So here is a person whose resources for offering public address come from the Bible.

But the third question we have to ask when giving witness to our faith is:

"What are we giving witness to?"

Is it from our own experience or are we pointing beyond ourselves to a God who acts in history?

If you look back now on the first and second paragraphs of the second inaugural address, it is as if Lincoln is somehow standing above or outside of the conflict.

He is like a chronicler.

He is describing the events.

In that central paragraph, there is a ringing affirmation - the Almighty has his own purposes.

And now we find Lincoln suggesting that the chief actor in the Civil War is God himself.

The Almighty has his own purposes.

The greatest tragedy of the Civil War, in a personal sense for Lincoln, was the death of his four year old son, Willie Lincoln.

He died in February of 1862 and Lincoln invited Phineas Densmore Gurly to come and preach the funeral sermon.

And while he was there, Gurly said to a grieving Abraham and Mary something that he called very comforting.

He encouraged them to get a clear and scriptural view of providence.

The second inaugural address is one of clear and scriptural providence.

When we come to the last paragraph, the one in which we are most familiar, we hear Lincoln's words that echo down through the century:

"... with malice toward none and charity for all."

Forty-one days after he delivered this address, he would be dead.

The people in Washington, struggling to know how to honor their fallen President, put on silk mourning badges.

Most of which bore this message:

"... with malice toward none, with charity for all."

For they had looked back at the prison of his death and understood that Lincoln had lived his life with malice toward none, with charity for all.

The real heart of the address is when to the surprise of everyone, he thunders forth sort of like a Puritan Jeremiah:

"... if we shall suppose that American slavery is one of those offenses which in the providence of God must needs come."

In this moment of high expectation, Lincoln dared to say to those assembled:

"We have a great evil in our midst."

The crowd would have cheered if he would have said, "southern slavery," or maybe if he even had said, "slavery," but he uses in inclusive language, "American slavery."

We are all involved in this terrible evil.

But then Lincoln comes to his close.

The indicative is like Paul's letters in the New Testament and then **Ephesians 4:1**:

"Therefore, I, a prisoner of the Lord, lead you to a life of the calling to which you have been called."

Abraham Lincoln:

"Therefore, with malice toward none, with charity for all."

I have thought for a long time how Lincoln may have come to those words, or whether he thought that a nation so deeply divided was actually able to come forward in acts of forgiveness, passion, and reconciliation.

We live in a divided nation today and part of the way we give witness to our faith is to listen to others speak from a Biblical standpoint and to point to a God that acts in history and then our words become our deeds as we live out the Christian calling with malice toward none and charity for all.

These are the words that reach across 140 years and are so strangely and beautifully timeless for us after all of these years.

Abraham Lincoln always read out loud.

Abraham would read to Mary.

Mary would read to Abraham.

I suggest in reading about Lincoln, we say and read his words out loud.

Listen for the word of God.

Listen for Abraham Lincoln.

"Fellow-Countrymen, at this second appearing to take the oath of the Presidential office there is less occasion for an extended address than there was at the first. Then a statement somewhat in detail of a course to be pursued seemed fitting and proper. Now, at the expiration of four years, during which public declarations have been constantly called forth on every point and phase of the great contest which still absorbs the attention and engrosses the energies of the nation, little that is new could be presented. The progress of our arms, upon which all else chiefly depends, is as well known to the public as to myself, and it is, I trust, reasonably satisfactory and encouraging to all. With high hope for the future, no prediction in regard to it is ventured.

On the occasion corresponding to this four years ago all thoughts were anxiously directed to an impending civil war. All dreaded it, all sought to avert it. While the inaugural address was being delivered from this place, devoted altogether to saving the Union without war, insurgent agents were in the city seeking to destroy it without war--seeking to dissolve the Union and divide effects by negotiation. Both parties deprecated war, but one of them would make war rather than let the nation survive, and the other would accept war rather than let it perish, and the war came.

One-eighth of the entire population were colored slaves, not distributed generally over the Union, but localized in the southern part of it. These slaves constituted a peculiar and powerful interest. All knew that this interest was somehow the cause of the war. To strengthen, perpetuate, and extend this interest was the object for which the insurgents would rend the Union even by war, while the Government claimed no right to do more than to restrict the territorial enlargement of it. Neither party expected for the war the magnitude or the duration which it has already attained. Neither anticipated that the cause of the conflict might cease with or even before the conflict itself should cease. Each looked for an easier triumph, and a result less fundamental and astounding. Both read the same Bible and pray to the same God, and each invokes His aid against the other. It may seem strange that any men should dare to ask a just God's assistance in wringing their bread from the sweat of other men's faces, but let us judge not, that we be not judged. The prayers of both could not be answered. That of neither has been answered fully.

The Almighty has His own purposes. "Woe unto the

world because of offenses; for it must needs be that offenses come, but woe to that man by whom the offense cometh." If we shall suppose that American slavery is one of those offenses which, in the providence of God, must needs come, but which, having continued through His appointed time, He now wills to remove, and that He gives to both North and South this terrible war as the woe due to those by whom the offense came, shall we discern therein any departure from those divine attributes which the believers in a living God always ascribe to Him? Fondly do we hope, fervently do we pray, that this mighty scourge of war may speedily pass away. Yet, if God wills that it continue until all the wealth piled by the bondsman's two hundred and fifty years of unrequited toil shall be sunk, and until every drop of blood drawn with the lash shall be paid by another drawn with the sword, as was said three thousand years ago, so still it must be said "the judgments of the Lord are true and righteous altogether.

With malice toward none, with charity for all, with firmness in the right as God gives us to see the right, let us strive on to finish the work we are in, to bind up the nation's wounds, to care for him who shall have borne the battle and for his widow and his orphan, to do all which may achieve and cherish a just and lasting peace among ourselves and with all nations.

NOTES

Interlude IV

In the late 1600's in colonial Boston, the celebration of Christmas was against the law.

Indeed, anyone evidencing the Spirit of Christmas could be fined five shillings.

In the early 1800's, Christmas was better known as a season for rioting in the streets and civil unrest.

However, in the mid-1800's, some interesting things changed the cultural response to the feast and, in 1870, Christmas was declared a federal holiday.

What happened?

American Christmas demonstrates the amazing influence of literature on a culture.

In 1819, best-selling author Washington Irving wrote a series of stories about the celebration of Christmas in an English manor house.

The sketches feature a squire who invited the peasants into his home for the holiday.

In contrast to the problems faced in American society, the two groups mingled effortlessly.

In Irving's mind, Christmas should be a peaceful, warm-hearted holiday bringing groups together across lines of wealth or social status.

Irving's fictitious celebrants enjoyed ancient customs including the crowning of a Lord of Misrule.

Irving's book, however, was not based on any holiday celebration he had attended – in fact, many historians say that Irving's account invented tradition by implying that it described the true customs of the season.

Another piece of literature perhaps more influential was later written by Charles Dickens' titled,

"A Christmas Carol."

For the American cultural celebration of Christmas largely began through the popularity of Dickens' classic story.

That same fact, though, accounts for much of the non-religious aspects of America's celebration.

"A Christmas Carol," does not overlook the birth of Christ.

It presumes the religious aspects of the day and its presence is woven throughout every part of the storyline.

There is a brief mention of Bob Cratchit and his son, Tiny Tim, attending Church on the day.

But it was not this part of the story that caught the popular imagination.

All told, it was the spirit of Christmas that sold America on the importance of the day.

Dickens wrote in the depths of the Victorian era.

That period was marked, both in England and America, by a rise of romanticism and a popular sentimentality for traditions and customs.

The century before had been dominated by the Enlightenment when all things rational ruled the day.

Indeed, it is not incorrect to see the sentimentality of the Victorian period as a reaction to the coldness of reason.

It was the figurative swing and sway of the cultural pendulum.

America's religious history has been a conflicted mix since the very beginning.

The New England colonies (among the earliest) were settled largely by Puritans, dissenters from the Church of England, who wanted a radical reform of English Christianity.

Unable to achieve their desires in England, they came to America and established their Churches here.

They opposed Church festivals and frivolities of almost every sort.

Their strict and dour form of Christianity waned and morphed over the decades.

English Churches outside of the Catholic and Anglican were non-liturgical.

Thus, the growth of a popular Christmas in the mid to late 19th century took place outside the walls of the Church.

It became a cultural holiday, with an emphasis on

family and the home.

Surprisingly, Christmas is probably far more a part of Church life in America today than at any time in our history.

But the echoes of cultural Christmas remain strong.

When Christmas Day falls on a Sunday, Christianity in America revisits its conflicted past.

It is not unusual to see Churches cancelling Sunday services, deferring to Christmas as a "family" celebration.

For liturgical Churches (Catholic, Orthodox, Anglican, Lutheran, etc.) such a practice seems scandalous in the extreme.

I might note, however, that the power of Christmas as an event in our culture, is rooted in the culture rather than the Church.

This is not a presumption about what should be.

Cultures are what they are and got that way by their peculiar history.

There are protests against the secular Christmas that say,

"Put the Christ back in Christmas!"

Another suggestion I might make is to,

"Put the Dickens back in Christmas."

The moral of Dickens' story:

Christmas is well-kept by a life of generosity and kindness.

That dear story is one of profound repentance, the healing of relationships, and the righting of wrongs.

Dickens' Christmas was synonymous with a life lived in accordance with the gospel.

He said it well at the end of his story:

Bob Cratchit was incredibly surprised, and so were many people who found Scrooge so changed.

Scrooge became a better person.

To Tiny Tim, who did not die, he was a second father.

Scrooge became as good a friend, as good a master, and as good a man, as the good old city knew, or any other good old city or town in the world could know.

It was always said of Scrooge, that he knew how to keep Christmas well. May that be honestly said of us, and all of us!

I absolutely think that Christmas should be a time for Christians to gather in Church to give thanks for the birth of Christ.

But outside its doors, no one of us could do better than Scrooge.

The busy-ness of Christmas, as well as the business of Christmas, could do well to listen to the words of Scrooge's partner, Jacob Marley, the tortured soul doomed to wander the world in chains.

Scrooge observed to him that he was always a good man of business.

Marley replied:

"Business!" cried the Ghost, wringing its hands again.

"Mankind was my business. The common welfare was my business; charity, mercy, forbearance, and benevolence, were, all, my business. The dealings of my trade were but a drop of water in the comprehensive ocean of my business!"

Would that such business was as popular as the tinsel and trees.

Thank you, Charles Dickens, for having said it all so well.

NOTES

Interlude V

On Christmas day nearly a half-century ago, Dr. Martin Luther King, Jr. stood before his congregation in Atlanta and preached his final Christmas sermon.

Four months later he would be assassinated in Memphis, Tennessee.

I had never heard this sermon before.

Never read it.

Or learned about it in any of my history classes.

Dr. King's foresight on the interdependency and the interconnectedness of a globalized world should stop readers in their tracks.

As we face global realities and fears, Dr. King roots us in our humanity and the better nature within ourselves.

Read Dr. King's sermon aloud to your family and children and remember the dream we must realize in the days ahead:

"Peace on Earth...

This Christmas season finds us a rather bewildered human race. We have neither peace within nor peace without. Everywhere paralyzing fears harrow people by day and haunt them by night. Our world is sick with war; everywhere we turn we see its ominous possibilities. And yet, my friends, the Christmas hope for peace and goodwill toward all men can no longer be dismissed as a kind of pious dream of some utopian. If we do not have goodwill toward men in this world, we will destroy ourselves by the misuse of our own instruments and our own power. Wisdom born of experience should tell us that war is obsolete. There may have been a time when war served as a negative good by preventing the spread and growth of an evil force, but the very destructive power of modern weapons of warfare eliminates even the possibility that war may any longer serve as a negative good. And so, if we assume that life is worth living, if we assume that mankind has a right to survive, then we must find an alternative to war — and so let us this morning think anew on the meaning of that Christmas hope: "Peace on Earth, Good Will toward Men." And as we explore these conditions, I would like to suggest that modern man really go all out to study the meaning of nonviolence, its philosophy, and its strategy.

We have experimented with the meaning of nonviolence in our struggle for racial justice in the United States, but now the time has come for man to experiment with nonviolence in all areas of human conflict, and that means nonviolence on an international scale.

Now let me suggest first that if we are to have peace on earth, our loyalties must become ecumenical rather than sectional. Our loyalties must transcend our race, our tribe, our class, and our nation; and this means we must develop a world perspective. No individual can live alone, and as long as we try, the

126

more we are going to have war in this world. Now the judgment of God is upon us, and we must either learn to live together as brothers or we are all going to perish together as fools.

Yes, as nations and individuals, we are interdependent. I have spoken to you before of our visit to India some years ago. It was a marvelous experience; but I say to you this morning that there were those depressing moments. How can one avoid being depressed when one sees with one's own eyes evidence of millions of people going to bed hungry at night? How can one avoid being depressed when one sees with one's own eyes thousands of people sleeping on the sidewalks at night? More than a million people sleep on the sidewalks of Bombay every night; more than half a million sleep on the sidewalks of Calcutta every night. They have no houses to go into. They have no beds to sleep in. As I beheld these conditions, something within me cried out:

"Can we in America stand idly by and not be concerned?"

And an answer came:

"Oh, no!"

And I started thinking about the fact that right here in our country we spend millions of dollars every day to store surplus food; and I said to myself:

"I know where we can store that food free of charge — in the wrinkled stomachs of the millions of God's children in Asia, Africa, Latin America, and even in our own nation, who go to bed hungry at night."

It really boils down to this: that all life is interrelated. We are all caught in an inescapable network of mutuality, tied into a single garment of destiny. Whatever affects one directly, affects all indirectly. We are made to live together because of the interrelated structure of reality. Did you ever stop to think that you cannot leave for your job in the morning without being dependent on most of the world? You get up in the morning and go to the bathroom and reach over for the sponge, and that is handed to you by a Pacific islander. You reach for a bar of soap, and that is given to you at the hands of a Frenchman. And then you go into the kitchen to drink your coffee for the morning, and that is poured into your cup by a South American. And maybe you want tea: that is poured into your cup by a Chinese. Or maybe you are desirous of having cocoa for breakfast, and that is poured into your cup by a West African. And then you reach over for your toast, and that is given to you at the hands of an English-speaking farmer, not to mention the baker. And before you finish eating breakfast in the morning, you have depended on more than half of the world. This is the way our universe is structured; this is its interrelated quality. We are not going to have peace on earth until we recognize this basic fact of the interrelated structure of all reality.

Now let me say, secondly, that if we are to have peace in the world, men and nations must embrace the nonviolent affirmation that ends and means must cohere. One of the great philosophical debates of history has been over the whole question of means and ends. And there have always been those who argued that the end justifies the means, that the means really are not important. The important thing is to get to the end, you see.

So, if you're seeking to develop a just society, they say, the important thing is to get there, and the means are really unimportant; any means will do so long as they get you there — they may be violent, they may be untruthful means; they may even be unjust means to a just end. There have been those who have argued this throughout history. But we will never have peace in the world until men everywhere recognize that ends are not cut off from means, because the means represent the ideal in the making, and the end in process, and ultimately you can't reach good ends through evil means, because the means represent the seed and the end represents the tree.

It is one of the strangest things that all the great military geniuses of the world have talked about peace. The conquerors of old who came killing in pursuit of peace, Alexander, Julius Caesar, Charlemagne, and Napoleon, were akin in seeking a peaceful world order. If you will read Mein Kampf closely enough, you will discover that Hitler contended that everything he did in Germany was for peace. And the leaders of the world today talk eloquently about peace. Every time we drop our bombs in North Vietnam, President Johnson talks eloquently about peace. What is the problem? They are talking about peace as a distant goal, as an end we seek, but one day we must come to see that peace is not merely a distant goal we seek, but that it is a means by which we arrive at that goal. We must pursue peaceful ends through peaceful means. All of this is saying that, in the final analysis, means and ends must cohere because the end is preexistent in the means, and ultimately destructive means cannot bring about constructive ends.

Now let me say that the next thing we must be concerned about if we are to have peace on earth and goodwill toward men is the nonviolent affirmation of the sacredness of all human life. Every man is somebody because he is a child of God. And so when we say "Thou shalt not kill," we're really saying that human life is too sacred to be taken on the battlefields of the world. Man is more than a tiny vagary of whirling electrons or a wisp of smoke from a limitless smoldering. Man is a child of God, made in His image, and therefore must be respected as such. Until men see this everywhere, until nations see this everywhere, we will be fighting wars. One day somebody should remind us that, even though there may be political and ideological differences between us, the Vietnamese are our brothers, the Russians are our brothers, the Chinese are our brothers; and one day we've got to sit down together at the table of brotherhood. But in Christ there is neither Jew nor Gentile. In Christ there is neither male nor female. In Christ there is neither Communist nor capitalist. In Christ, somehow, there is neither bound nor free. We are all one in Christ Jesus. And when we truly believe in the sacredness of human personality, we won't exploit people, we won't trample over people with the iron feet of oppression, we won't kill anybody.

There are three words for "love" in the Greek New Testament; one is the word eros. Eros is a sort of esthetic, romantic love. Plato used to talk about it a great deal in his dialogues, the yearning of the soul for the realm of the divine. And there is and can always be something beautiful about eros, even in its expressions of romance. Some of the most beautiful love in all of the world has been expressed this way.

Then the Greek language talks about philos, which is another word for love, and philos is a kind of intimate love between personal friends. This is the kind of love you have for those people that you get along with well, and those whom you like on this level you love because you are loved.

Then the Greek language has another word for love, and that is the word agape. Agape is more than romantic love, it is more than friendship. Agape is understanding, creative, redemptive good will toward all men. Agape is an overflowing love which seeks nothing in return. Theologians would say that it is the love of God operating in the human heart. When you rise to love on this level, you love all men not because you like them, not because their ways appeal to you, but you love them because God loves them. This is what Jesus meant when he said, "Love your enemies." And I'm happy that he didn't say, "Like your enemies," because there are some people that I find it pretty difficult to like. Liking is an affectionate emotion, and I can't like anybody who would bomb my home. I can't like anybody who would exploit

131

me. I can't like anybody who would trample over me with injustices. I can't like them. I can't like anybody who threatens to kill me day in and day out. But Jesus reminds us that love is greater than liking. Love is understanding, creative, redemptive goodwill toward all men. And I think this is where we are, as a people, in our struggle for racial justice. We can't ever give up. We must work passionately and unrelentingly for first-class citizenship. We must never let up in our determination to remove every vestige of segregation and discrimination from our nation, but we shall not in the process relinquish our privilege to love.

I've seen too much hate to want to hate, myself, and I've seen hate on the faces of too many sheriffs, too many white citizens' councilors, and too many Klansmen of the South to want to hate, myself; and every time I see it, I say to myself, hate is too great a burden to bear. Somehow we must be able to stand up before our most bitter opponents and say:

"We shall match your capacity to inflict suffering by our capacity to endure suffering. We will meet your physical force with soul force. Do to us what you will, and we will still love you. We cannot in all good conscience obey your unjust laws and abide by the unjust system, because noncooperation with evil is as much a moral obligation as is cooperation with good, and so throw us in jail and we will still love you. Bomb our homes and threaten our children, and, as difficult as it is, we will still love you. Send your hooded perpetrators of violence into our communities at the midnight hour and drag us out *on some wayside road and leave us half-dead as you beat us, and we will still love you. Send your propaganda agents around the country, and make it appear that we are not fit, culturally and otherwise, for integration, and we will still love you. But be assured that we will wear you down by our capacity to suffer, and one day we will win our freedom. We will not only win freedom for ourselves; we will so appeal to your heart and conscience that we will win you in the process, and our victory will be a double victory."*

If there is to be peace on earth and goodwill toward men, we must finally believe in the ultimate morality of the universe and believe that all reality hinges on moral foundations. Something must remind us of this as we once again stand in the Christmas season and think of the Easter season simultaneously, for the two somehow go together. Christ came to show us the way. Men love darkness rather than the light, and they crucified Him, and there on Good Friday on the Cross it was still dark, but then Easter came, and Easter is an eternal reminder of the fact that the truth-crushed earth will rise again. Easter justifies Carlyle in saying, "No lie can live forever." And so this is our faith, as we continue to hope for peace on earth and goodwill toward men: let us know that in the process we have cosmic companionship.

In 1963, on a sweltering August afternoon, we stood in Washington, D.C., and talked to the nation about many things. Toward the end of that afternoon, I tried to talk to the nation about a dream that I had had, and I must confess to you today that not long after talking about that dream I started seeing it turn into a nightmare. I remember the first time I saw that dream turn into a nightmare, just a few weeks after I had talked about it. It was when four beautiful, unoffending, innocent Negro girls were murdered in a church in Birmingham, Alabama. I watched that dream turn into a nightmare as I moved through the ghettos of the nation and saw my black brothers and sisters perishing on a lonely island of poverty in the midst of a vast ocean of material prosperity, and saw the nation doing nothing to grapple with the Negroes' problem of poverty. I saw that dream turn into a nightmare as I watched my black brothers and sisters in the midst of anger and understandable outrage, in the midst of their hurt, in the midst of their disappointment, turn to misguided riots to try to solve that problem. I saw that dream turn into a nightmare as I watched the war in Vietnam escalating, and as I saw so-called military advisors, 16,000 strong, turn into fighting soldiers until today over 500,000 American boys are fighting on Asian soil. Yes, I am personally the victim of deferred dreams, of blasted hopes, but in spite of that I close today by saying I still have a dream, because, you know, you can't give up in life. If you lose hope, somehow you lose that vitality that keeps life moving, you lose that courage to be, that quality that helps you go on in spite of all. And so today I still have a dream.

I have a dream that one day men will rise up and come to see that they are made to live together as brothers. I still have a dream this morning that one day every Negro in this country, every colored person in the world, will be judged on the basis of the content of his character rather than the color of his skin, and every man will respect the dignity and worth of human personality. I still have a dream that one day the idle industries of Appalachia will be revitalized, and the empty stomachs of Mississippi will be filled, and brotherhood will be more than a few words at the end of a prayer, but rather the first order of business on every legislative agenda. I still have a dream today that one day justice will roll down like water, and righteousness like a mighty stream. I still have a dream today that in all of our state houses and city halls men will be elected to go there who will do justly and love mercy and walk humbly with their God. I still have a dream today that one day war will come to an end, that men will beat their swords into plowshares and their spears into pruning hooks, that nations will no longer rise up against nations, neither will they study war any more. I still have a dream today that one day the lamb and the lion will lie down together and every man will sit under his own vine and fig tree and none shall be afraid. I still have a dream today that one day every valley shall be exalted and every mountain and hill will be made low, the rough places will be made smooth and the crooked places straight, and the glory of the Lord shall be revealed, and all flesh shall see it together. I still have a dream that with this faith we will be able to adjourn the councils of despair and bring new light into the dark chambers of pessimism. With this faith we will be able to speed up the day when there will be peace on earth and goodwill toward men. It will be a glorious day, the morning stars will sing together, and the sons of God will *shout for joy."*

<u>NOTES</u>

Interlude VI

The Bible teems with monsters.

From the Leviathan with its fearful scales and claws, to the Behemoth with brass-like bones and cedar-strong tail.

In a vision, Daniel encountered four great beasts:

"One like a lion with eagle's wings, one like a bear with three ribs in its mouth, another like a leopard with four wings and four heads, and a fourth with iron teeth, bronze claws, and ten horns." <u>Daniel 7</u>

The book of Revelation combines these images into a description of a single monster rising from the sea, resembling a leopard, lion, and bear, with,

"Seven heads and ten horns, and upon his horns ten crowns. <u>Revelation 13:1</u>

The beast is joined by a fearsome consort:

A fiery-red dragon whose tail thrashes so widely it sweeps a third of the stars from the sky.

Biblical beasts can represent several things.

The awe-inspiring mystery of the natural world.

The fearful chaos of the unknown.

The sovereignty of God over even the most powerful forces in the universe.

But in the case of the mutant creatures of Daniel and

Revelation, they represent the evils of oppressive empires.

It is easy for modern-day readers to forget that much of the Bible was written by religious minorities living under the heels of powerful nation-states known for their extravagant wealth and violence.

For the authors of the Old Testament, it was the Egyptian, Assyrian, Babylonian, Greek, and Persian Empires.

For the authors of the New Testament, it was, of course, the massive Roman Empire.

These various superpowers, which inflicted centuries of suffering upon the Jews and other conquered populations, became collectively known among the people of God as Babylon.

One of the most important questions facing the people who gave us the Bible was:

"How do we resist Babylon, both as an exterior force that opposes the ways of God and an interior pull that tempts us with imitation and assimilation?"

They answered with volumes of stories, poems, prophecies, and admonitions grappling with their identity as an exiled people, their anger at the forces that scattered and oppressed them, God's role in their exile and deliverance, and the ultimate hope that one day,

"Babylon, the jewel of kingdoms, the pride and glory of the Babylonians, will be overthrown by God" Isaiah 13:19.

It is in this sense that much of Scripture qualifies as resistance literature.

It defies the empire by subverting the notion that history will be written by the wealthy, powerful, and cruel.

Insisting instead that the God of the oppressed will have the final word.

Throughout the Bible's resistance stories, we encounter examples of apocalyptic literature.

The word apocalypse means 'unveiling' or 'disclosing'.

An apocalyptic event or vision, therefore, produces and opportunity for exposure to revelation.

It peels back the layers of pomp and pre-tense, fear, and uncertainty, to expose the true forces at work in the world.

Using a composition of symbolic and theologically charged language, the authors of scripture employ apocalyptic literature to dramatize the work of the Resistance, in efforts to offer hope to those suffering under the weight of an empire that seems, on the surface, all-powerful and unassailable.

So, when the prophets Daniel and John envision the empires as vicious beasts, what they are saying is:

"Beneath all the wealth, power, and excess of these dazzling empires lie grotesque monsters, trampling everyone and everything in their path."

And when they depict God as tolerating, then

restraining, and finally destroying these monsters, what they are saying is:

"The story isn't over; even the greatest empires are no match for goodness, righteousness, and justice. It might not look like it now, but the Resistance is winning."

The beasts of Daniel and Revelation do not need to be literal to be real.

To the people who first read the Bible, they were as real as the imperial soldiers who marched down their streets, the royal edicts that threatened their homes and livelihoods, and the heavy fear that crept into every fitful dream.

The Bible is not a book of teasers in which God has buried secrets only to be revealed three millennia later.

Rather, apocalyptic texts proclaim that a guiding hand controls history, and assure that justice will prevail.

When you belong to the privileged class of the most powerful global military superpower in the world, it can be hard to relate to the oppressed minorities who wrote so much of the Bible.

The fact is, the shadow under which most of the world trembles today belongs to America, and its beasts could be named any number of things - White Supremacy, Colonialism, the Prison Industrial Complex, the War Machine, Civil Religion, Materialism, Greed, etc.

America's no ancient Babylon or Rome.

But America is no kingdom of God either.

If you doubt it, study an old diagram of a slave ship.

Try to count the number of chained-up bodies drawn flatly in the cargo hold, and multiply that by hundreds of thousands, representing the nearly half a million Africans brought to America in the slave trade.

Then remember that each of those bodies represents the very real life of a very real human being, created in the image of God, with memories and ideas and quirks and fears, and that those who survived the voyage across the Middle Passage were brutally enslaved by people who claimed to love God.

Or consider the Trail of Tears, and try to imagine what it would be like to be a Cherokee mother, driven out of your home by the US government, stripped of your belongings, and forced to walk thousands of miles with your children without enough food or medical care.

Or study the history of child labor in the United States.

Or research the treatment of the intellectually and/or developmentally disabled in institutions termed 'lunatic-asylums'.

Or Japanese internment during World War II.

Or Jim Crow.

Or the nine hundred Jewish refugees aboard the St.

Louis who were turned away from the United States and sent back to Europe to face the Holocaust.

The fact is, despite wistful nostalgia for the days when America was supposedly,

"One nation under God," the history of this country is littered with the bodies of innocent men, women, and children who were neglected, enslaved, dispossessed, and slaughtered so the privileged class could have a surplus of abundant resources.

More land.

More money.

More power.

More status.

More guns, more profits, more amenities, more square footage, more security, more fame, etc.

And these are not just phantoms of the past.

Having been historically dispossessed and discriminated against, African American and indigenous communities continue to face higher rates of poverty and crime, and struggle disproportionately for access to quality education, healthy food, secure housing, and affordable health care.

While the ultra-rich get richer, middle and lower-income wages have stagnated, resulting in an increase of Working Poor in America.

In many states, you can still get fired from your job

for simply being a homosexual.

However, you can be a serial womanizer who gets caught secretly bragging about assaulting women and still get elected President of the United States of America.

There is just no denying that the very things for which Israel was condemned by the prophets remain potent and prevalent sins in our culture.

These sins are embedded in nearly every system of our society.

We are all culpable and responsible for working towards change.

Yet rather than confessing our sins, and rather than dismantling the systems that perpetuate them, many Christians shrug it off as part of an irrelevant past or spin out religious-sounding rhetoric about peace and reconciliation without engaging in the hard work of repentance and restitution.

The quick-fix culture commands the oppressed to just move on and let the injustice go.

I have heard many preachers liken the church's response to racism in America to the words of Jeremiah, who cried,

*"They dress the wound of my people as though it were not serious. 'Peace, peace,' they say, when there is no peace."*Jeremiah 6:14

Saying we are a nation of peace doesn't make it so!

Not for Trayvon Martin, not for Tamir Rice, not for

the twenty kindergartners shot at Sandy Hook Elementary School, and certainly not for that Cherokee mother.

Tensions around issues of injustice must not be avoided in the name of an easy peace and cheap grace, but they must rather be passionately engaged.

"Until justice flows down like a river, righteousness like a never-failing stream."

For too long, the American church has chosen the promise of power over prophetic voice.

We have allied ourselves with the empire and created more of them.

We have, consciously and unconsciously, done the bidding of the Beast.

Therefore, it is so important to follow the lead of modern-day prophets like Bree Newsome who, in scaling that flagpole and removing the Confederate flag, declared God's reign over and above the tradition of prophetic protest.

Her actions helped my generation visualize a better future.

She simultaneously revealed things as they are and how they might be.

These are the people telling today's resistance stories, drawing from the Bible's deep well of prophetic examples for inspiration and strength.

Though political, they avoid partisanship.

Though clear-eyed, they remain stubbornly hopeful.

What I love about the Bible is that the story is not over.

There are still prophets in our midst.

There are still dragons and beasts.

It might not look like it, but the Resistance is winning.

The light is breaking through.

So, listen.

Listen to the voices crying from the wilderness.

They are pointing us to a new King and a better kingdom.

As Jesus said,

"Let those with ears, hear."

NOTES

Interlude VII

I often look back and think of Samuel Logan Brengle, who became one of the first great leaders of the Salvation Army in the United States in the early 1900's.

The Salvation Army had been established in London by General William Booth at the end of the 1800s.

And Samuel Logan Brengle, who had had a great education in both Indiana and Boston, said,

"I'm going to throw it all away. I'm going to London to care for the poor with William Booth."

And people thought he was foolish, but it was his sovereign choice to decide what to with the rest of his life.

I also often reflect on Mother Teresa and her Sisters of Charity serving the poorest of the poor in Calcutta.

In essence, she became like them so that she could serve them more effectively.

So, the following question is haunting on all kinds of levels:

If I were a real Man or Woman of Faith, wouldn't I give it all away too?

Let the wind take it away?

The floods take it away?

And shouldn't I be overjoyed to do just that?

Well the whole idea to me seems to be powerful and plausible, though I must admit I become a bit anxious when we are considering giving EVERYTHING away.

Can't I just keep a little for the journey?

Historically, it may seem to be compelling.

It may even raise doubts about whether Jesus wants us to do that seems almost to be self-serving - as if we're trying to wiggle out of what Jesus says explicitly and clearly.

Until we take the story that we have read and juxtapose it with other stories that the Bible shares with us.

Then we discover that most of the Saints in the scriptures have not given it all away by any means.

The first is a story that we often share with children, but it is for adults as well.

It is the story of Zacchaeus in **Luke 19**.

This man has made a lot of money and he has done it by cheating other people.

He is a Jewish tax collector whom collects taxes from his own people while secretly doing it on behalf of the Romans who have conquered the land.

They told their tax collectors that they wanted them to collect a certain amount of money, but that they could collect it however they wanted - skimming and stealing from innocent people as long as they delivered payment on time.

He beats and cheats other people until they give him everything he wants and then a lot more.

And he becomes very wealthy by doing so.

So, Zacchaeus, for some odd reason, wants to see the beloved Jesus as He passes through Jericho.

Upon arriving to Jesus' ministry, he is unable to get a glimpse of the teacher because of the large crowd.

So, Zacchaeus climbs a tree to see Jesus above the crowd.

Well, as Jesus notices Zacchaeus and tells him that He would like to visit his residence.

He spends time with Zacchaeus, and when they emerge from the house, Zacchaeus makes a proclamation to the people outside.

He states that he will make restitution four-fold.

Somehow, through his conversation with Jesus, Zacchaeus has found a freedom to be generous.

And then he says,

"As for the rest, I will give half to the poor."

This is pretty significant:

"...half..."

But what is important to notice is that Jesus does not turn on him and say,

"That is not enough! You need to give it all away!"

Jesus doesn't do that.

Indeed, He makes a wonderful statement.

When Jesus sees what Zacchaeus does with his money He says,

"Today salvation has come to this house."

It is a beautiful statement that God would say to you and me:

"Today salvation has come to this house."

Jesus says this because He could see that Zacchaeus has been liberated from the neediness of a life esteemed in self.

Not because he gave so much, but because Jesus could see that something changed in his heart.

Sacrificial giving indeed, but not giving all of it away.

And there is a second story that helps answer a question which bothered me when I was younger:

If Jesus gives everything away, how does He survive with His disciples as He preaches and teaches?

What does He depend on to eat and live?

The answer is found in this little vignette in **Luke 8**.

It tells the story very briefly of the fact that there were some women who traveled with the crowd and cared for them out of their means.

Among the many that helped provide for Jesus were

Mary Magdalene, Joanna the wife of Chusa, Herod's steward, and Suzanna.

In Greek, the word 'provide' is in the imperfect tense, which means it is continuous:

Which basically means they didn't let it all go at once and kept providing for Jesus and His Disciples.

They held onto it and they distributed it over time in order to support the ministry of Jesus.

To make sure that it was sustained and that it thrived and flourished over the long haul.

And that is far and away the pattern we see most clearly in the pages of scripture when it comes to wealth.

Not only in Jesus' ministry but throughout the whole Bible:

We have been given what we have.

Everything has and will be given to us by God.

We have been given what we have so that we can support, sustain, and expand God's work in the world.

The call is not to let it go all at once, but to let it go step-by-step, piece-by-piece, systematically, thoughtfully, and prayerfully.

We have let it all go for the glory of God and ultimately for the building up of His kingdom here on Earth.

Through that kind of systematic giving, our lives are

changed and transformed, and we actually become different people.

Not that we set out to be generous, but that we have developed long term practices in our lives which change us and turn us into the people God wants us to be.

After all, on your tombstone what do you want written there more than anything else?

Thinking of my own tombstone:

"Emmanuel had a lot. Made a lot. Got a lot."

Or,

"Emmanuel gave a lot. Emmanuel was a giver. Emmanuel was a lover"

Isn't that what we want others to think of us when our day comes?

"This person was a lover and a giver; generous, joyful for the cause of God and the blessing of many human beings."

My life has been spent helping people learn the gift of giving.

After years in this pursuit I have come to reveal:

"The happiest people on Earth are the people who learn the joy of giving."

I say that after having seen it experienced by thousands of people in thousands of ways.

I heard it in the voice of a businessman who had

made a commitment to give half of a million dollars to help build a new sanctuary for his church.

He later told me that nothing he had ever done in his life had meant as much to him as that decision to stretch himself in the giving process.

Over the years I have come to appreciate more and more the model of generosity set before me by my parents.

Before my mother became ill with breast cancer, she volunteered what time she could at a local church.

We went to church and we were expected to put our offering in the envelope.

My father bought new clothes and gifts for coworker's children who could not afford them.

These lessons carried over into the world around us.

No one in need was ever turned away from our door.

Giving was a way of life in the Abbott household.

I thank them for setting that example in the joy of giving.

And that is a theme that he follows through in the rest of this book.

"THE HAPPIEST PEOPLE ON EARTH ARE THE PEOPLE WHO HAVE LEARNED THE JOY OF GIVING."

The happiest people on earth are the people who believe that everything we possess comes from God.

That God really is the provider.

It is not ours anyway.

We are a pass-through account and we have been called to manage it wisely as it passes through our lives and on to someone or something else in the name of God.

We are stewards.

We are His hands and feet.

We are His body on earth.

In a sense of humility, He depends on us to carry out His ministry on earth.

And He says,

"I want you to share in this through what you give with your body and with your resources, with your stuff and with your money."

We need others around us to witness the unexplainable blessings that God has in store for us.

This principle in the pages of scripture is what we call a tithe – one-tenth.

Some are already there; some need to go higher while some give more than they keep.

Wherever we are, we need to take what we have and offer it to God and say,

"Lord, you're in control of this, and of me. What is it you want me to do?"

I think, ultimately, that is what that young, wealthy and powerful gentleman could not say nor do.

It was not just a matter of giving it all away.

It was a matter of the fact that he really did believe that he owned it.

It was his and he could not open his life to God as Jesus wanted him to do.

I believe the Apostle Paul's words, though, can speak to all of us.

He writes to the **Corinthians**,

"Do as you have made up your mind. Not under compulsion but willingly. For God loves a cheerful giver."

God is looking for the person who not only gives cheerfully but for the person who finds joy in the process and purpose in the privilege of giving.

God insatiably desires ALL of us:

Our heart, our mind, and our souls.

Even our temptations, and definitely our intentions.

He wants us to give Him the permission to conduct His ministry through us, flowing into the lives of others.

And in so doing, find more joy and peace and fulfillment than we could ever begin to imagine.

<u>NOTES</u>

Interlude VIII

We like to paint Mary in the softer hues.

Her robes clean.

Hair combed and covered.

Constantly poised in prayerful surrender.

On the contrary, this young woman was a fierce one.

Full of strength and fury.

When she accepts the dangerous charge before her, Mary offers a prophecy:

"My soul magnifies the Lord, and my spirit rejoices in God my Savior, for He has looked with favor on the lowliness of His servant. Surely, from now on all generations will call me blessed; for the Mighty One has done great things for me, and Holy is His name. His mercy is for those who fear Him from generation to generation. He has shown strength with His arm; He has scattered the proud in the thoughts of their hearts. He has brought down the powerful from their thrones and lifted up the lowly; He has filled the hungry with good things and sent the rich away empty. He has helped His servant Israel, in remembrance of His mercy, according to the promise He made to our ancestors, to Abraham and to his descendants forever." **Luke 1:46-55**

When sung in a warm, candlelit congregation, it can be easy to blunt these words.

To imagine them as symbolic and comforting.

However, I heard a prophecy less sentimental.

I was feeling angry and restless.

And so, in this season I heard Mary's Magnificat shouted.

Not sung.

In the halls of the Capitol Building:

"He has filled the hungry with good things and sent the rich away empty."

In the corridors of the West Wing:

"He has brought down the powerful from their thrones and lifted up the lowly."

In the streets of Charlottesville:

"He has shown strength with His arm; He has scattered the proud in the thoughts of their hearts."

Among women who have survived assault, harassment, and rape:

"He has looked with favor on the lowliness of His servant. Surely, from now on all generations will call me blessed."

Among the poor, the refugees, the victims of gun violence, and the faithful ministers of the gospel who at great cost are speaking out against the false religions of nationalism and white supremacy:

"His mercy is for those who fear Him, from

generation to generation."

With the Magnificat, Mary not only announces a birth, she announces the inauguration of a New Kingdom.

One that stands in stark contrast to every other kingdom.

Past, present, and future.

With the Magnificat, Mary declares that God has indeed chosen sides.

And it is not with the powerful - but the humble.

It is not with the rich - but with the poor.

It is not with the occupying force - but with people on the margins.

This is the stunning claim of the incarnation:

"God has made a home among the very people the world casts aside."

And in her defiant prayer, Mary, a refugee and a religious minority in an occupied land, names this reality:

"God is with us. And if God is with us, who can stand against us?"

Such a sentiment stands in blasphemous contradiction to the very doctrine of incarnation we are meant to embrace.

Incarnation is not about desperately grasping at the threads of power and privilege.

It is about surrendering, setting aside, and finding God in the vulnerability.

To claim that this country is, ' The Home of the Free', while its powerful systematically oppress the poor, turn away refugees, incite violence against religious and ethnic minorities, is, in the words of the prophet Amos, *sickening* to God.

"I hate, I despise your festivals and I take no delight in your solemn assemblies... Take away from me the noise of your songs; I will not listen to the melody of your harps. But let justice roll down like waters, and righteousness like an ever-flowing stream." <u>Amos 5</u>

And so, I am awaiting with the angst of the prophets.

With the restlessness of the psalmist who cried,

"How long, oh Lord, will You hide your face forever?"

With the stubborn, unsentimental hope of a woman so convinced that the baby in her womb would change everything.

She proclaimed in present tense:

The powerful have already been humbled.

The vulnerable have already been lifted up.

For God has made a home among the people.

God has made a home with us.

NOTES

Interlude IX

In Elizabeth Barrett Browning's poem 'Aurora Leigh,' she writes:

"Earth's crammed with heaven, And every common bush afire with God."

So here is what I wonder.

What if burning bushes are not as rare as we anticipated?

Maybe the burning bush is not unique to Moses.

The rabbis said that others passed by the bush while it was burning, but only Moses turned aside.

What if the miracle of the burning bush is not that it was not consumed by the fire, but that Moses turned aside?

Maybe turning aside to see this thing is the real miracle of this story.

What if the burning bush is a part of each of our lives?

Maybe the only question is whether we will turn aside.

What if every burning bush is a call asking for and awaiting a response from us?

The question is:

Will we turn aside and respond to the call being

made upon us?

Burning bushes are those circumstances or events that interrupt life and grab our attention.

They are not part of our plans.

They take us by surprise.

They stop us in our tracks and cause us to turn aside.

We take a second look.

Burning bushes come to us as an overflow, sometimes in positive ways and other times not.

Regardless of how it comes to us, the burning bush shatters the horizon of our expectation.

There is risk and potential for instability.

Moses never thought it possible for a bush to be on fire but not be burned up.

He never expected or planned on being the one to bring God's people out of Egypt.

Those were beyond his horizon of expectation.

In each of our lives there are experiences that shatter our horizon of expectation.

They are events, conversations and words, happenings that were unplanned, unexpected, unforeseeable, and they always ask something of us, a response.

They are those times that leave us weeping and asking,

"Why?"

They are those experiences when the excess is overwhelming, and we have no words.

Only tears of joy.

They are those times when we cannot wait to share with someone what has happened and we say,

"Not in my wildest dreams could I have imagined or guessed that this would be my life."

They are those times when we shake our head in disbelief and say,

"No, that's not possible; it can't be."

And sometimes we throw up our hands and say,

"God only knows."

When and how has any of this happened in your life?

What have been the burning bushes for you?

The scriptures give us a litany of burning bushes:

The Tower of Siloam falling.

The suffering of the Galileans at the hands of Pilate.

The fig tree that produced no fruit.

Each circumstance shatters a horizon of expectation.

That does not mean, however, that God caused those things to happen.

It means that God calls in every place and situation.

God calls with the promise of life, more life, new life.

One that is already prepared!

And each call awaits a response.

The burning bush does not reveal God to be a Supreme Being, a Superhero, or the Big Guy in the Sky.

Instead it reveals God to be more like a suggestion or an insistence.

God says to Moses,

"I have observed the misery of my people." "I have heard their cry." "I know their suffering, and I have come down to deliver them from the Egyptians."

God is coming to rescue God's people.

But listen to what God says next to Moses:

"So come, I will send you to Pharaoh to bring my people, the Israelites, out of the land of Egypt." "I have come down to deliver them," God says. "So come, I will send you," God says to Moses.

God is going to deliver His people by sending Moses.

Moses is to give existence to God's call for deliverance.

Moses works God's will into reality.

What if that's how God is working in our lives too?

Do you remember that the rabbis said others passed

by the burning bush but did not turn aside?

What if they too were to have given existence to God's suggestions or insistence that the Israelites be freed from Egypt?

I wonder if they would have turned aside given that information.

When have we failed or refused to respond to the call on our lives?

The burning bush story is one of call and response.

Something is being called for in the name of God.

Something is being asked of us in the name of God.

The burning bush experience does not happen apart from everyday life.

Moses was keeping the flock of his father in law when he turned aside at the sight of the burning bush.

He was doing the ordinary routine.

In what ways is the horizon of your expectation being shattered today?

It could be as ordinary as a fig tree that produces no fruit, as tragic as a falling tower, and everything in between.

What is interrupting your life today and asking for a response?

What is being called for?

How will you respond?

This is where I often get stuck:

On the response.

What is the right response?

I always want to get it right.

But what if there isn't one right answer?

Will we know for sure?

What if the 'right' response is whatever brings forth life, more life, and new life?

And what if that looks different in each of our lives?

The vineyard owner responds to the barren fig tree by wanting to cut it down.

The gardener responds by wanting to fertilize the tree.

The text, however, does not tell us who is right or what happens next.

What if both are right?

What if being right isn't even the measure?

Maybe life is the only measure.

And Moses?

How does Moses know if he will get it right?

He doesn't.

He doesn't know any more than we do.

There will, however, be a sign.

The sign, God says, will come after the people have been delivered.

Not before.

It is as if God is saying,

"You will look back on all this and see I was there all along."

And isn't that an accurate description of life?

We live life forward, uncertain, and not knowing, but we only begin to understand and make sense of it in retrospect.

What if there are no guarantees?

What if the best thing we can do is to rely on hope, love and faith?

What if that is how we approached every burning bush in our life?

And what if we saw every common bush afire with God?

<u>NOTES</u>

Interlude X

We all have Nazareth's in our lives.

They are the objects of our judgments, assumptions, and exclusion.

They are the people, places, and situations from which we neither expect nor see the possibility of anything good coming.

Certainly, nothing beneficial to us.

Nazareth is about how we see and relate to others, whether in foreign policy or in our own communities.

Nathanael's question is not unique to him.

It gets asked every day.

Nathanael's question, however, is not really about Nazareth.

It is about Nathanael.

That is true for all of us despite the differences between what or whom our Nazareth might be.

That question says more about us than it does Nazareth.

It is about our belief and unbelief.

It is about our biases, prejudices, and fears.

It is about our wounds, losses, and sorrows.

It is about our guilt and shame.

It is about the assumptions and judgments we make.

It is about all the many filters through which we see the world, others, ourselves, and God.

Somehow, we become convinced that there is no way anything good could come from there (or here).

But what if that is exactly how it is?

What if God reveals Himself through the one who is different?

The stranger?

For us, Nazareth is a blind spot and a hardening of our heart.

For God, however, Nazareth is a place of epiphany.

A place where God shows God's self and invites us to see, to believe, and to love in new ways.

Isn't that what happened for Nathanael?

He let go of one belief to hold a new belief.

He walked away from the fig tree of his assumptions to consider something new and change his direction, which in turn changed his destiny.

He left behind his certitudes about Nazareth to give his attention to something unexpected.

Nathanael was willing to reconsider and open himself to a new belief.

And what he saw and experienced simply did not fit

his assumptions or the judgments he had made.

It totally exceeded his expectations.

How many times has that happened to us?

We make a statement, a judgment, or an assumption about someone or something before we truly understand.

When that happens, we realize once again that Nazareth is not about the other person but about the condition of our own heart.

Nazareth is not about another's economic value to us but about the willingness of our heart to value another human being.

Nazareth is not about how much power another has but about our choosing to empower and support the lives of those around us.

Nazareth is not about a religion, a race, a nationality, a sexual orientation, economic or immigration status - but about Emmanuel.

God is with every human being regardless of who they are or where they come from.

Nazareth is real.

It is flesh and blood real.

It is the recognition that your flesh and blood,

My flesh and blood,

The flesh and blood of strangers,

The flesh and blood of Nathanael,

And flesh and blood of Jesus are all the flesh and blood of God.

And maybe that is the challenge and difficulty surrounding Nazareth.

Sometimes it is so ordinary and so much like everyday life that we just do not see it.

We become blind to it.

Other times it hits so close to home and asks so much of us that we refuse to see it.

We close our eyes and turn away in denial.

Regardless of the differences in each of our Nazareth's, there is always an invitation.

It is the invitation to rise and change direction.

To leave behind our assumptions and judgments.

To give up our certitudes.

To risk not knowing.

To see with the eyes of our heart.

And to let ourselves be surprised by God.

That choice is always before us.

It is a choice we make every time we see the face of another.

It is a choice we make every time we hear the news or read the headlines.

It is a choice we make every time we look out on the world from beneath our own fig tree.

Can anything good come out of Nazareth?

I can't answer that question for you, and you can't answer it for me.

Philip could not answer it for Nathanael.

Neither could Jesus.

If we really want to know the answer to that question, then we must discern and decide for ourselves.

Nathanael did and it changed his life forever.

What about us?

Can anything good come out of our Nazareth?

"Come and see."

NOTES

Interlude XI

Whatever house you enter, first say,

"Peace to this house." <u>Luke 10:5</u>

It feels as though it was just the other day that our hearts were torn for the victims of the Orlando Massacre.

And not too long after that, the attack in Istanbul.

Then, twenty-eight people died in an attack on a Bangladeshi cafe.

I remember waking up one bright and early morning:

I checked the news and car bombs in Baghdad had killed 126 people.

These are just tragedies that captured major headlines.

There are others that do not even make the news, though they are no less important, no less painful, and no less tragic.

Some are global, some are national, and some are personal.

If these events have left us heartbroken and weeping - imagine what God must be seeing and feeling.

The Creator, who entrusts us with His creation, with one another's lives, and with His own life.

Today, the Creator and the created once again stand together.

Weeping and brokenhearted.

I no longer see these tragedies as problems to be fixed or behaviors to be corrected.

That approach has not gotten us far.

Rather, I view them as symptoms pointing to a deeper issue.

Until we are willing to deal with the deeper issue things are not likely to change.

The deeper issue is the human heart.

Whether by a terrorist attack, through prejudice and discrimination against a minority group, in our political campaigns, or in our personal relationships.

The violence and mistreatment we perpetrate on each other arise first from an inner violence that poisons and fragments the human heart.

We need a change of heart.

We need a heart at peace.

I cannot help but ask,

"Where is the peace of God today?"

I think that is a question many are asking.

It is a question I suspect God might also be asking.

The blood of the victims, the tears of the mourners, and the pain of the world cry and beg for a different answer.

Let us not give the same old answers.

Let us not use the same old excuses.

Let us not offer the same old solutions.

Let us not meet the world with the same old beliefs.

Instead, let us become people with hearts at peace.

Not at comparison.

Isn't that what you want for yourself?

For your family and friends?

For your children and grandchildren?

For the world?

If the events of today's world offer us anything at all, it is the opportunity to rethink what peace means and reorient our hearts.

So, let me ask you this:

What does peace mean to you?

What comes to mind when you think of peace?

What does it look like?

What shape does it take?

Are you willing to let go of that understanding of peace?

Are you willing to change your understanding and consider something else?

Are you willing to pay the price for peace?

I am not asking about our willingness to risk the lives of our military men and women or increase the military's budget.

We have already proven our willingness to do that.

I am asking about our willingness to change our understanding and practice of peace.

I believe most of us have an understanding of peace that is miniscule and much too narrow.

We limit peace to a particular set of behaviors and usually they are the behaviors we expect or want from the other person.

We think of peace as an ideal to be attained and we define it as the absence or elimination of conflict.

We have convinced ourselves that peace will come when this person or that group changes.

Ultimately, we condition peace on our ability to change or control another.

How often does Jesus instruct us to go and change other people?

He does not.

That may be our way, but it is definitely not His way.

Jesus does, however, spend a lot of time teaching us to change ourselves and our way of being toward another.

The struggle for peace begins within us.

So, let us consider what a heart at peace might look like.

What if a heart at peace is about loving our neighbor as we love ourselves?

A heart at peace refuses to lump masses of unknown people into lifeless categories such as Republican, Democrat, conservative, liberal, LGBQT, Muslim, etc., and make them objects to be dealt with or enemies to be defeated.

A heart at peace encounters everyone as a person.

It looks another in the face and recognizes itself.

So, tell me, what do you see when you look in the face of another?

What if a heart at peace offers forgiveness to our enemies?

Are we willing to do that?

What if a heart at peace means feeding the hungry, giving drink to the thirsty, clothing the naked, and visiting the sick or imprisoned?

We must regard the needs and desires of another as important as our own.

We must refuse to betray ourselves and refuse to horriblize others.

Peace does not begin with our behaviors, but with our perception.

Our seeing each other as human beings created in the image and likeness of God.

Our behavior toward one another will be determined by our way of being toward one another.

If our hearts are constantly at comparison - it makes no difference how polite we are to each other.

Violence is present.

Offering the peace of God is more than a friendly handshake and a warm hug.

It is the recognition of another's existence and their value as a human being, regardless of whether they are family, friend, stranger, or enemy.

The peace of God is a practice to be lived every moment of every day of our lives.

That means practicing peace with our friends and family.

It means practicing peace with our enemies.

It means practicing peace with the stranger, with those who are different from us, and with those who believe different from us.

"Whatever house you enter, first say, 'Peace to this house.'"

NOTES

Interlude XII

I have sometimes quipped that children are born lawyers.

Children reveal our instinct for fairness, the root concept in the virtue of justice.

Of course, as every parent knows, that instinct is often distorted, with the desire for a narcissistic fairness.

Justice is a virtue with deep, visceral content.

Whenever it is invoked, it should be accompanied with flags of warning.

Of all the virtues, it is the least able to stand alone.

Paired with the instinct for fairness, these virtues quietly blend with the sin of envy and the desire that someone should 'get what's coming to them'.

It is never satisfied with fairness – it requires punishment.

When we take pleasure in another's misfortune, it is not the virtue of justice – it is the sin of envy.

It is quite rare in our world that we find justice standing alone, pure, and undefiled.

The desire for justice alone can easily become an instrument of great evil.

The natural appetite for justice knows no limit.

The quiet virtues of temperance and prudence are the necessary antidotes to such excess.

They are also much less easily acquired because they require ascetical efforts.

Temperance is best described as self-control.

Prudence is the foundation of wisdom.

Though both are natural to us, both require nurture and development.

Temperance and prudence are least evident in the young – it takes time and exposure for us to grow in experience.

It is the context of a virtuous community that allows such experience to safely bear fruit.

No human being stands alone.

The virtues are formed and shaped in the context of community.

However, if it is not acquired early, it can be difficult to acquire at all (as noted in cases of "feral" children).

Temperance and prudence involve the ability to say,

"No."

Not just to others, but to ourselves.

Temperance and prudence are also the hardest to measure and define.

What is the proper amount of self-control?

What should be avoided or encouraged?

Those decisions point to prudence as perhaps the queen of virtues.

Knowing what the right amount is, at the right time, and the right manner, is the most difficult thing of all.

Prudence is a stern rebuke of our youth-oriented culture.

Since approximately the 1950's, we have been an economic culture that directs its markets towards youth.

What is described as 'fashionable' is almost entirely defined by what sells best among the young.

The psychology of such marketing has long been a part of American consumer capitalism.

Refined today by algorithms of artificial intelligence.

We have created an economy that thrives on inexperience, intemperance, and poor judgement.

The results speak for themselves.

It is only in those who are experienced that temperance and prudence can be found.

Of course, experience alone does not teach – there is a broader consensus across time that must be acquired and later confirmed in experience.

The only thing that has not been done throughout history is to live as though the past has nothing to teach us.

The nature of tradition and its role in the formation of virtue differs from mere conservatism.

Conservatism is more than just the resistance to change.

Receiving a tradition is a matter of a living relationship with what has gone before and recognizing its place in the present.

Conservatism treats the past as important – tradition treats the past as still present.

In a certain manner, modernity is the abrogation of temperance and prudence.

For example, no single invention has had more impact on current culture than the smart phone.

It makes the invention of the printing press pale in comparison.

Modernity, as a philosophy, has had little regard for what has come before.

It imagines that human beings live best when they are allowed to freely choose their actions.

Choice is certainly a part of life, but it has been exalted to an absurd degree.

We do not choose our language, our DNA, the culture into which we are born, nor the family in which we grow up.

Indeed, almost everything that constitutes who a person is comes from something that is not chosen.

Choices are tiny variations on a theme that was

already set in place.

How well we live those variations will depend upon character.

Both our own, and that of others around us.

When the inherited wisdom of tradition is interrupted in a society, what is handed down is truly a gift from God.

Our reception of what is given can be diminished, but the source of all virtue can also restore what has been lost.

In every generation, there are those who embody what it is to be virtuous.

In some cases, we call them saints.

In other cases, we call them teachers, friends, helpers.

In every case, to know them is to be touched by heaven.

NOTES

Interlude XIII

Philippians is part of a collection called Paul's Prison Epistles (his three other epistles were Ephesians, Colossians, and Philemon).

Paul was a man familiar with suffering, which he reminds us of in **2 Corinthians 11:24-28**:

"Five times I received from the Jews the forty lashes minus one. Three times I was beaten with rods, once I was pelted with stones, three times I was shipwrecked, I spent a night and a day in the open sea, I have been constantly on the move. I have been in danger from rivers, in danger from bandits, in danger from my fellow Jews, in danger from Gentiles; in danger in the city, in danger in the country, in danger at sea; and in danger from false believers. I have labored and toiled and have often gone without sleep; I have known hunger and thirst and have often gone without food; I have been cold and naked. Besides everything else, I face daily the pressure of my concern for all the churches."

Amidst the turmoil and pain, Paul excavated a sublime treasure available to us:

Joy.

During this two-year period, Paul was on house arrest.

Although, he was permitted to receive guests and teach freely.

"Paul and Timothy, servants of Christ Jesus, To all God's holy people in Christ Jesus at Philippi, together with the overseers and deacons: Grace and peace to you from God our Father and the Lord Jesus Christ. I thank my God every time I remember you. In all my prayers for all of you, I always pray with joy because of your partnership in the gospel from the first day until now, being confident of this, that He who began a good work in you will carry it on to completion until the day of Christ Jesus. It is right for me to feel this way about all of you, since I have you in my heart and, whether I am in chains or defending and confirming the gospel, all of you share in God's grace with me."

Paul names the Siamese twins of the Bible:

Grace and peace.

Grace precedes peace.

You cannot experience the unshakeable peace of God without first accepting His gift of grace.

As you begin your relationship or embark on strengthening it, receive God's unmerited favor toward you and move onward with freedom from burden.

Trust that His work on this earth, and on the cross, was enough to provide a life that is,

"Exceedingly abundantly above all that we ask or think, according to the power that works in us, to Him be the glory" (Ephesians 3:20-21).

Read no further until that message of grace is established in your heart.

It is not your work; it is Christ's work for you and in you.

Paul learned how to change his mind, so God could change his heart.

"God can testify how I long for all of you with the affection of Christ Jesus. And this is my prayer: that your love may abound more and more in knowledge and depth of insight, so that you may be able to discern what is best and may be pure and blameless for the day of Christ, filled with the fruit of righteousness that comes through Jesus Christ - to the glory and praise of God."

Paul shares exactly what his prayer is towards:

Abound in love, gain more knowledge, discern what is best, and be filled with righteous fruit.

If you separate these ingredients a bit more, you will notice it begins with love.

Let us ask God to teach us to love how He loves.

The result is radical – and we know from **Galatians 5:22-23** that the fruit of the spirit is love.

That means that joy, peace, patience, kindness, goodness, faithfulness, gentleness, and self-control are all byproducts of love.

"Now I want you to know, brothers and sisters, that what has happened to me has actually served to advance the gospel. As a result, it has become clear

throughout the whole palace guard and to everyone else that I am in chains for Christ. And because of my chains, most of the brothers and sisters have become confident in the Lord and dare even more to proclaim the gospel without fear. It is true that some preach Christ out of envy and rivalry, but others out of goodwill. The latter do so out of love, knowing that I am put here for the defense of the gospel. The former preaches Christ out of selfish ambition, not sincerely, supposing that they can stir up trouble for me while I am in chains."

Verse 12 includes a statement we should inscribe into our hearts as we face life's circumstances:

"...What has happened to me has actually served to advance the gospel."

When my mother was experiencing being treated for stage three metastatic breast cancer, she shared with me a few heartfelt words and it aligns well with verse 12:

""Abba, Father," He cried out, "everything is possible for you. Please take this cup of suffering away from me. Yet I want your will to be done, not mine." <u>Mark 14:36</u>

If it is going to happen, the Father must allow it.

Absolutely ANYYTHING and EVERYTHING is possible for the Master of the Universe.

Even when it is dark and seemingly hopeless, we can trust that it is for our good and His glory.

""But what does it matter?" The important thing is

that in every way, whether from false motives or true, Christ is preached. And because of this I rejoice. Yes, and I will continue to rejoice, for I know that through your prayers and God's provision of the Spirit of Jesus Christ what has happened to me will turn out for my deliverance."

Verse 18 implies there were some individuals more concerned with creating a following than with preaching the message of Christ.

Isn't that the truth today?

With social media platforms and living life online, it is incredibly easy to portray a false image instead of unabashedly proclaiming the unadulterated truth.

Lord, keep our motives pure and our eyes fixed, fastened, and focused.

"I eagerly expect and hope that I will in no way be ashamed but will have sufficient courage so that now as always Christ will be exalted in my body, whether by life or by death. For to me, to live is Christ and to die is gain. If I am to go on living in the body, this will mean fruitful labor for me. Yet what shall I choose? I do not know! I am torn between the two: I desire to depart and be with Christ, which is better by far; but it is more necessary for you that I remain in the body. Convinced of this, I know that I will remain, and I will continue with all of you for your progress and joy in the faith, so that through my being with you again your boasting in Christ Jesus will abound on account of me."

In case we are apt to elevate Paul to a pedestal of

divinity, verse 20 reveals his fleshly tendencies:

"I eagerly expect and hope that I will in no way be ashamed, but will have sufficient courage..."

By reading between the lines, this tells us that Paul experiences fear when it comes to preaching the gospel.

What we cannot afford to miss is what Paul does in anticipation of the fear:

He expects the good, he hopes for the best, and he takes courage in knowing God will be sufficient in the moment.

Paul's mind-set toward his time on this Earth is stellar.

While he had no spouse or children, he did have fellow believers whom he loved like sons, such as Timothy, Titus, and Onesimus.

Even though Paul viewed himself as their spiritual father, it did not cast a shadow on his view of the heavenly.

"Whatever happens, conduct yourselves in a manner worthy of the gospel of Christ. Then, whether I come and see you or only hear about you in my absence, I will know that you stand firm in the one Spirit, striving together as one for the faith of the gospel without being frightened in any way by those who oppose you. This is a sign to them that they will be destroyed, but that you will be saved—and that by God. For it has been granted to you on behalf of Christ not only to believe in Him, but also to suffer

for Him, since you are going through the same struggle you saw I had, and now hear that I still have."

Whatever happens in the future, let us choose to conduct ourselves in a manner worthy of the gospel of Christ.

We are never promised that we will have a life of rainbows and unicorns once we choose to follow Him.

With brevity, we are told we will have trouble.

However, we are given the hope of knowing Christ has overcome the world, which means that on that final day, we will be at Christ's side.

Let us live expectantly, hopefully, and with great courage.

Amen.

NOTES

Interlude XIV

When we live to seek our glory and are willing to do whatever it takes to get ahead, we are bound to fall.

But if we succeed in surrendering our ambition to God's purposes, we will help others find their way on the path of life.

That is exactly what Paul was about to do.

Paul had letters in hand from the high priest authorizing the arrest of followers of the Way.

He began travelling on the road to Damascus.

While on the road, he was stopped in his tracks, and his life was changed forever.

Here is how he described the experience:

"I was traveling to Damascus with the authority and commission of the chief priests, when at midday along the road . . . I saw a light from heaven, brighter than the sun, shining around me and my companions. When we had all fallen to the ground, I heard a voice saying to me in the Hebrew language, "Saul, Saul, why are you persecuting me? It hurts you to kick against the goads." I asked, "Who are you, Lord?" The Lord answered, "I am Jesus whom you are persecuting." <u>Acts 26:12-15</u>

Some have suggested the light from heaven was a bolt of lightning that struck near Paul.

Whatever happened, it was terrifying, and Paul was

blinded by it.

In the midst of the light, Paul heard Jesus speaking to him.

I love what Jesus said:

"Saul, Saul...it hurts you to kick against the goads."

What on earth is a goad?

A goad is a stick with a pointed end, used to prod oxen and cattle to move in the direction their owner wants them to go.

Jesus was saying, in essence, that He had been prodding Paul in the right direction for some time, that Paul had not paid attention, and that his failure to pay attention was hurting Paul and others.

What an interesting idea.

God is prodding us on a regular basis, seeking to lead us, guide us, and move us to live out His will.

God's prod is gentle yet persistent.

And God further allows us to resist his goading.

Paul, temporarily blinded, was led by his fellow travelers to Damascus.

This lion of a man, whom had breathed murderous threats against the church of Jesus, was now terrified.

Paul sat there for three days.

He was unwilling to eat or drink.

God was working on him in the silence as he came

face to face with a disturbing fact:

His desire to serve God had been distorted by his own ambition, which had led him to persecute God's people.

Meanwhile, God was 'goading' someone else - a man named Ananias who was a follower of Christ and someone whom Paul likely had come to arrest.

Christ spoke to Ananias in a vision.

We are not told the precise nature of this prod, perhaps it was a dream, an idea, a strong urging from within, or a still small voice.

"The Lord said to him, "Get up and go to the street called Straight, and at the house of Judas look for a man of Tarsus named Saul."...But Ananias answered, "Lord, I have heard from many about this man, how much evil he has done to your saints.""
Acts 9:11-13

Christ told Ananias to track down Paul and pray for him so that his eyesight would be restored.

Understandably, Ananias was afraid and objected, still afraid that Paul was a murderer.

But the voice of Christ persisted, so finally Ananias went.

Imagine the courage it must have taken for Ananias to confront Paul the Inquisitor.

"Ananias went and entered the house. He laid his hands on Saul and said, "Brother Saul, the Lord Jesus, who appeared to you on your way here, has

sent me so that you may regain your sight and be filled with the Holy Spirit." And immediately something like scales fell from his eyes, and his sight was restored. Then he got up and was baptized."
<u>Acts 9:17-18</u>

Notice that Paul's conversion was a result both of his experience of Christ and of Ananias sharing with him.

This is how it often works.

Most of us do not have a blinding-light conversion, but we do experience Christ in some way.

We feel Him speaking to us, we sense His love, and we feel moved with compassion.

And we also have individuals like Ananias' who come to offer us revelation.

We never again hear about Ananias in the Bible.

He courageously stepped up and shared Christ with Paul.

And as a result, he changed the world.

As for Paul, he learned that conversion happens to us when we stop pursuing our own blind ambitions.

When we recognize God's prodding in our lives.

And when we finally surrender to God's will.

That is where the real adventure begins.

It certainly began there for Paul.

NOTES

Interlude XV

"Paul, a prisoner of Christ Jesus, and Timothy our brother, To Philemon our dear friend and fellow worker - also to Apphia our sister and Archippus our fellow soldier - and to the church that meets in your home." <u>Philemon 1:1-2</u>

In this prison epistle, Paul writes a letter to Philemon - a wealthy man from Colossae.

Apphia was most likely Philemon's wife, and Archippus his son.

The wives typically oversaw slaves, so this letter was addressed to her as well.

"Grace and peace to you from God our Father and the Lord Jesus Christ." <u>Philemon 1:3</u>

In Paul's usual fashion, he speaks of the Siamese Twins of the Bible:

Grace and peace.

Grace precedes peace.

You cannot experience the unshakeable peace of God without first accepting His gift of grace through Christ Jesus.

"Trust that His work on this earth, and on the cross, was enough to provide a life that is "exceedingly abundantly above all that we ask or think, according to the power that works in us, to Him be the glory."" <u>Ephesians 3:20-21</u>

"I always thank my God as I remember you in my prayers, because I hear about your love for all his holy people and your faith in the Lord Jesus. I pray that your partnership with us in the faith may be effective in deepening your understanding of every good thing we share for the sake of Christ. Your love has given me great joy and encouragement, because you, brother, have refreshed the hearts of the Lord's people." <u>Philemon 1:4-7</u>

If there is anything, we have learned studying Paul's prison epistles, it is that he is a prayer warrior!

He was in continual conversation with God, and his heart overflowed with the love of Jesus.

I like how it says,

"...your partnership with us in the faith..."

If we genuinely want others to have a deepened understanding of Christ, we must recognize that we need each other.

I need you.

Your uniqueness; your engagement; and your words of love.

And you need me.

My encouragement; my hard truths; and my words of love.

We need each other because we are all living life together.

"Therefore, although in Christ I could be bold and

order you to do what you ought to do, yet I prefer to appeal to you on the basis of love. It is as none other than Paul - an old man and now also a prisoner of Christ Jesus - that I appeal to you for my son Onesimus, who became my son while I was in chains. Formerly he was useless to you, but now he has become useful both to you and to me."
<u>Philemon 1:8-11</u>

Even though Paul had the respect and authority to command Philemon to release Onesimus, he chose rather to appeal to him in love.

Onesimus' name translates to 'useful' in Greek.

I am sure Philemon felt Onesimus was a useless servant.

Paul states, in verse 11, that while Onesimus may have once been useless, he now knows Christ and is transformed.

There is a beautiful parallel in this verse.

While we can runaway from Christ, He continuously pursues us with His kindness.

We are sacred instruments created specifically for His glory.

Let Him orchestrate a captivating melody using your life.

"I am sending him—who is my very heart—back to you. I would have liked to keep him with me so that he could take your place in helping me while I am in chains for the gospel. But I did not want to do

anything without your consent, so that any favor you do would not seem forced but would be voluntary. Perhaps the reason he was separated from you for a little while was that you might have him back forever— no longer as a slave, but better than a slave, as a dear brother. He is very dear to me but even dearer to you, both as a fellow man and as a brother in the Lord."<u>Philemon 1:12-16</u>

Paul could have kept Onesimus, but he knew the right thing to do was to send him back to his owner.

It is tough when the right thing is so hard on the heart.

It is clear from Paul's use of words that he deeply loved Onesimus, but he understood that Philemon owned Onesimus.

During the Roman Empire, there were tens of thousands of slaves.

It was not unusual for a slave to be crucified for escaping.

Which is why Paul pleads with Philemon to have mercy on Onesimus, as if Philemon were handling Paul's own heart.

May we show the same mercy to others because we know Christ has lavished us with His own unwarranted mercy.

Paul wanted Philemon to receive Onesimus not as a slave, but as a brother in the Lord.

This reminds me of Jesus' words in <u>John 15:15</u>,

"I no longer call you servants because a servant does not know his master's business. Instead, I have called you friends, for everything that I learned from my Father I have made known to you."

I am so thankful Jesus is a friend of sinners, and I am one of them.

"So, if you consider me a partner, welcome him as you would welcome me. If he has done you any wrong or owes you anything, charge it to me. I, Paul, am writing this with my own hand. I will pay it back— not to mention that you owe me your very self. I do wish, brother, that I may have some benefit from you in the Lord; refresh my heart in Christ. Confident of your obedience, I write to you, knowing that you will do even more than I ask." <u>**Philemon 1:17-21**</u>

Paul says,

"I'll pay for Onesimus' sins."

The only way Paul could extend this depth of love is by receiving and recognizing the unconditional love Christ showed him on the road to Damascus.

Let us keep reminding ourselves of how much grace and mercy we have been shown, and in turn, allow it to pour over into our own relationships.

I can just hear Paul's words of inspiration to Philemon.

He is saying,

"I know you can do this. I know you will make the right choice because we serve the Lord Jesus Christ together. You and I are partners and we are bound by the eternal blood."

Maybe you need to hear that word for yourself.

I am certain you will make the God choice because greater is He who is in you than whatever you are up against.

Press in and press on.

"And one thing more: Prepare a guest room for me, because I hope to be restored to you in answer to your prayers. Epaphras, my fellow prisoner in Christ Jesus, sends you greetings. And so do Mark, Aristarchus, Demas and Luke, my fellow workers. The grace of the Lord Jesus Christ be with your spirit." <u>Philemon 1:22-25</u>

Every morning God whispers, in one form or another,

"Make room for me."

Is there space in your day?

Is it clutter-free so God has a place to sit?

Is He worth your time?

Is He worth your day?

Is He worth your life?

Christ died for you.

It is time to live for Him.

Amen.

NOTES

Interlude XVI

<u>Luke 24:13-39</u>

"Now that same day two of them were going to a village called Emmaus, about seven miles from Jerusalem. They were talking with each other about everything that had happened. As they talked and discussed these things with each other, Jesus Himself came up and walked along with them; but they were kept from recognizing Him.

He asked them, "What are you discussing together as you walk along?" They stood still; their faces downcast.

One of them, named Cleopas, asked Him, "Are you the only one visiting Jerusalem who does not know the things that have happened there in these days?"

""What things?" He asked. "About Jesus of Nazareth," they replied. "He was a prophet, powerful in word and deed before God and all the people. The chief priests and our rulers handed Him over to be sentenced to death, and they crucified Him; but we had hoped that He was the one who was going to redeem Israel. And what is more, it is the third day since all this took place. In addition, some of our women amazed us. They went to the tomb early this morning but did not find His body. They came and told us that they had seen a vision of angels, who said He was alive. Then some of our companions went to the

tomb and found it just as the women had said, but they did not see Jesus."

He said to them, "How foolish you are, and how slow to believe all that the prophets have spoken! Did not the Messiah have to suffer these things and then enter His glory?" And beginning with Moses and all the Prophets, He explained to them what was said in all the Scriptures concerning Himself."

As they approached the village to which they were going, Jesus continued on as if He were going farther. But they urged Him strongly, "Stay with us, for it is nearly evening; the day is almost over." So, He went in to stay with them.

When He was at the table with them, He took bread, gave thanks, broke it, and began to give it to them. Then their eyes were opened, and they recognized Him, and He disappeared from their sight. They asked each other, "Were not our hearts burning within us while He talked with us on the road and opened the Scriptures to us?"

They got up and returned at once to Jerusalem. There they found the Eleven and those with them, assembled together and saying, "It is true! The Lord has risen and has appeared to Simon." Then the two told what had happened on the way, and how Jesus was recognized by them when He broke the bread.

While they were still talking about this, Jesus Himself stood among them and said to them, "Peace be with you."

They were startled and frightened, thinking they saw a ghost. He said to them, "Why are you troubled, and why do doubts rise in your minds? Look at my hands and my feet. It is I myself! Touch me and see; a ghost does not have flesh and bones, as you see I have.""

In the previous excerpt, the disciples were lugubrious and embarked to trek the seven-mile road back to their village.

They had seen all their hopes wiped away.

The great prophet whom they had followed as Messiah had been crucified.

It is clear from the conversation between them that they were now completely hopeless and utterly perplexed.

They certainly had not expected Jesus to be crucified, even more so, they were now hearing reports he had risen.

But dead men do not rise!?

So, what exactly was going on here?

Their dreams were shattered, and they were left to realize what it was all about as they walked home.

How do we know that?

By their own words to Jesus.

"He was a prophet, powerful in word and deed before God and all the people. The chief priests and our rulers handed Him over to be sentenced to

death, and they crucified Him; but we had hoped
that He was the one who was going to redeem Israel.
"

We know from the gospels that by the end of His
ministry, Jesus was becoming more explicit about
who He was and what was going to happen to Him.

So why was his death and resurrection so
unexpected?

Because to them, He was a great prophet, He was
the Messiah who had come to redeem Israel - but
not the Son of God.

They had heard Jesus' words, but they heard what
they wanted to hear in the context of what they
expected their Messiah to be.

So, they were going home rather than waiting in
Jerusalem to see what happened next.

The problem is that the two disciples had displaced
grace with merit.

When we start talking and thinking adventitiously -
we step back from a God who seeks to pour out his
blessings graciously on us to take the view that God is
capricious, hard to please and has profound
expectations beyond the laws of common decency.

What is the consequence of that kind of thinking?

Whenever life gets hard - when we struggle with
financial problems, family problems poor health,
stress, depression - we start thinking about God in a
way that is does not reflect His love, His grace, or

His mercy.

We think we have not been spiritual enough and begin to believe that we are not in his favor.

Or we begin to think we are not really saved - that we have somehow lost our salvation.

We blame him for dreadful things that happen to us.

Why did God take my friend, parent, sibling, husband, wife, and/or child?

I have been faithful, so why did God let this happen to me?

Why didn't God rescue me?

So, we rely on our own personal resources, our own wisdom and logic.

I know of many who were once faith-filled who have walked away from God because they feel let down or even exhausted.

How can we face the consequences of a fallen world, our personal failures, the failures of others that have an impact on us AND the evils of this world that beset us?

I think the answer is right here in this passage.

As these two disciples contemplate and are confused that their dreams are shattered - along comes Jesus.

For most people looking at this, the immediate question that jumps to mind is,

"How didn't they recognize him, as they obviously

knew him well?"

It is possible to be so tied up in our own problems that we never see God at work in our lives and the lives of others.

God is at work, but are we looking?

Or are we failing to see Him even though He is in plain sight?

It is more common than you think.

What I, as a minister, would like to focus on in my life mission is that God is at work in the world, in our nation, in our community, in our church and in our lives.

The problem is that we sometimes do not see it because we are preoccupied with our own stuff - or worse - we do not believe we are deserving to be blessed people, a blessed family, or a blessed community.

That is just not true!

We need to lift our eyes and see what God is doing now.

Referring to **Luke 24:16**, the failure of the disciples to recognize Jesus is more specific

"They were kept from recognizing Him."

It was the divine intention to conceal Jesus in plain sight by keeping their minds closed for a short while to serve His purposes which was to address their false understanding of who Jesus was.

They needed a major change in their way of thinking.

To have just seen Him there would have made certain that they learned nothing.

So, they remained blissfully ignorant of his identity.

Then, He said to them,

"How foolish you are, and how slow to believe all that the prophets have spoken! Did not the Messiah have to suffer these things and then enter His glory?" And beginning with Moses and all the Prophets, He explained to them what was said in all the Scriptures concerning Himself.

Not only had they not seen Jesus in plain sight - they had read their scriptures many times but had never seen the truth of God which was there in plain sight too.

Their testimony after Jesus was revealed was this:

"He opened to us the Scriptures."

The Greek word for opened is '*Dianoigo*'.

It means to open thoroughly, to interpret, or to explain.

Jesus opened their minds to what the word of God said - and it was all there.

They at last understood what Jesus stood for and the resurrection was a reality.

Dead men do rise, and Jesus was alive!

It was good hospitality to invite a fellow traveler into one's home for the night, as there were no torches or streetlights when it got dark and safety was indoors for the night.

At their meal, the guest broke bread - and that is when their eyes were opened.

They realized exactly who their companion had been - and then He was gone!

The look on their faces must have been priceless!

Why didn't Jesus stay and talk to them for longer?

Good question.

Because this story teaches us something vital down the ages.

We do not have Jesus with us to explain what He is about.

It is all there in God's word.

God has left us with everything we need to live Jesus' risen life!

How that is delivered to us has not changed.

We have the word of God, and we have the Holy Spirit who brings us the understanding that we need of the deep things of God:

"But it was to us that God revealed these things by His Spirit. For His Spirit searches out everything and shows us God's deep secrets. No one can know a person's thoughts except that person's own spirit, and no one can know God's thoughts except God's

own Spirit. And we have received God's Spirit, so we can know the wonderful things God has freely given us."

It is given for us to understand God.

It is the same process as the road to Emmaus.

But to do that we need to walk with Him - and we do that by reading His word and praying that it will be opened to us as we go through life.

Because when we do take it seriously and God speaks to us then this happens:

"Were not our hearts burning within us while He talked with us on the road and opened the Scriptures to us?"

What did they mean?

Jesus' words put fire in their bellies.

The Greek word '*Kaio*' means fire and it has different implications in the New Testament, including enlightenment.

As Jesus spoke, their hearts were lit up.

He had turned the spiritual lights on for them.

For the first time they saw from scripture, who Jesus was -why He came - why He died - the truth that He was now risen, alive!

Commentators often suggest the other uses of the Greek word for '*Kaio*' - cleansing (as in cauterizing) - in terms of refining us, burning up the dross, power, etc.

But the flame is also light, taking us from the darkness of ignorance into the truth and the light of God.

And the risen Jesus brings that fire He kindled in the disciples to us.

It is not something that needs to be earned or deserved.

We do not need to gain some level of spirituality.

It is offered to us.

Jesus says,

"Walk with me, listen and let the Holy Spirit ignite you - may your heart burn within you."

As we reflect on this passage, we think again of how we have so often responded to the pains and pressures of life similar to the two disappointed and confused disciples on the Emmaus road.

Yet, Jesus journeys with us.

He has left His word with us.

He has given us His Spirit so we may interpret and understand the deep revelations of God.

NOTES

Interlude XVII

It is interesting that the topic of virtue was the one matter on which Christians of the early Church and the educated pagans around them agreed.

Indeed, the list of virtues that came to be a hallmark of ascetic writings in the Fathers was pretty much the same list found earlier in the works of Plato, Aristotle, and the Stoics.

In general, what constituted virtue was much the same whether seen from the point of view of a Christian or a pagan philosopher.

The compact list of the virtues is instructive:

Prudence

The ability to discern the appropriate course of action to be taken in a given situation at the appropriate time

Courage

Fortitude, forbearance, strength, endurance, the ability to confront fear, uncertainty, and intimidation

Temperance

The practice of self-control, discretion, and moderation, tempering the appetites

Justice

Fairness, being equitable with others.

Religious experts added the 'theological virtues' to that earlier list:

Faith, hope, and love.

When we read of Roman soldiers being so deeply moved by the courage and faith of suffering martyrs that they renounced the gods and leapt into the arena in order to die with them, we are seeing a case of men who were already committed to courage and justice who would rather die with the innocent than be united with the wicked.

It is difficult to preach to those who have little virtue.

Virtue is a word that asks the question:

"What kind of person am I?"

Now let me ask you,

What kind of person leaps into an arena in order to die with the innocent?

What kind of person leaves everything he has in order to follow Christ?

What kind of person shares what he has with those who have less?

What kind of person speaks the truth when a lie would be richly rewarded?

Virtue is a way that we can measure faith in its depths.

It is not theological or educational sophistication that measures character – it is virtue.

I was well aware of my father's faults and had the temerity as a teen to point them out to him from time to time.

I could never have accused him of cowardice.

I do not say the same about prudence or temperance.

Those came slowly to him.

But he was the kind of man whose conscience would not be silenced for any reason of convenience.

Surely, he endured challenging times.

Some, like him, were never far from those times at any point in their lives.

What kind of people endure difficult challenges to their faith?

What kind of community fosters virtue in its members?

It is interesting to me, in thinking of C.S. Lewis and J. R. R. Tolkien, that they both lost their mothers when they were young.

Tolkien was orphaned, and Lewis was shipped off to horrible boarding schools.

When they met, Lewis was not yet a Christian.

However, I suspect that his character was already formed.

I do not think we can point to specific communities for how they became good men.

Oddly, I think we have to say that they read good books.

Many of those books were tales of ancient heroes.

What kind of community fosters virtue in its members?

First and foremost, I think, it is a community that tells good stories of good men and good women.

It is the task of the community both to tell and to become the relevant story.

The community is the sacrament of virtue and that place where every virtue finds its true home.

Character and virtue ask questions that have very little to do with success.

The greatest failures of Christianity in the modern world have not been failures to "succeed."

They have been failures of character, when "success" and worldly concerns have overwhelmed doing the right thing at the right time for the right reason.

God give us courage!

NOTES

Ab Initio

"When you see it, your heart will rejoice, and you will flourish like grass." -Isaiah 66:14

It was like a ship sailing the unknown, I had been at sea for so long.

Beginning to starve from the lack of food.

I heard stories about this glorious land across the vast unknown and I was determined to just set eyes upon it, so I knew it was real.

Never feeling, seeing, or hearing this privilege before, I truly had no clue what I was in search of.

What it looked like or where it originates from.

Out of plain view it was hidden.

Such as the rocks that claimed the vessel that brought me here.

Washed ashore and stripped of my pride and dignity, I stood before the woman I would call mine.

I had known it as soon as I saw her hand held out to comfort me in my time of inequity.

I just wish I never let go.

Desolation

Why does God allow suffering?

If I were an insurer or a lawyer, in a legal sense, I would be looking for blame.

Whose fault is it?

Who should pay?

Was someone negligent?

And if it was not - if it was a freak accident over which no-one had control then we are back to the God of the gaps – then it is an act of God!

Most of us at some time have asked the questions:

"Why has God done this to me?"

"Have I sinned and He's punishing me?

"How could a God of love do this to me, His child?"

"Why didn't God stop my loved one from dying - after all, He does do miracles from time to time?"

"Why didn't God do a miracle this time?"

This kind of thinking is all based on the idea of merit and gratification – that people should get what they deserve and if that is not in line with our expectations - then God is questioned or even blamed.

Although we have probably uttered many of those phrases at some time, they are all based on a faulty view of God.

God is indeed a God of love, grace, and mercy.

He is not an insolent, capricious over-ruler who causes pain and wishes for us to struggle, worry, or agonize.

There is no simple answer to our questions.

If I manage to satisfy everyone reading this, then I will be one of the first ministers in thousands of years to have achieved it anywhere.

My intention is to give you some things to pray about - think about - discuss with others - and allow the Holy Spirit to make sense of it for you.

If we want to get anywhere near answering the question, we need to go right back to the beginning of the Bible - to its foundation in **Genesis 1-3**.

For many it is a difficult passage.

The Bible is not a scientific book, yet people spend a lot of time on Genesis trying to equate it to modern science.

Literary experts look at the narrative and ask is this history or parable?

Archaeologists try to explore its historicity.

Most of all the Bible is a theological book, and the theology of Genesis is relatively straight-forward as it gives us the relationship between God and Humanity.

If we want to understand why human beings suffer,

then we need to start here.

"Then God said, "Let us make man in our image, after our likeness. And let them have dominion over the fish of the sea and over the birds of the heavens and over the livestock and over all the earth and over every creeping thing that creeps on the earth." So, God created man in His own image, in the image of God, He created Him; male and female, He created them. And God blessed them. And God said to them, "Be fruitful and multiply and fill the earth and subdue it and have dominion over the fish of the sea and over the birds of the heavens and over every living thing that moves on the earth." And God said, "Behold, I have given you every plant yielding seed that is on the face of all the earth, and every tree with seed in its fruit. You shall have them for food. And to every beast of the earth and to every bird of the heavens and to everything that creeps on the earth, everything that has the breath of life, I have given every green plant for food." And it was so."
<u>Genesis 1:26-31</u>

Humanity is given dominion over the planet – or more precisely, over life on the planet.

We say the creator is in control of His world - but right from the start of Genesis, we see humanity made in the image of God and given God's authority to rule.

We were given the knowledge, creativity, and the free will to make decisions for ourselves – to fill the Earth and subdue it.

That has never changed since God breathed life into

Adam.

We have the privilege to decide our own destiny here on Earth.

But there is another thing we learn about humanity in Genesis:

With free will comes responsibility for the actions we take.

Humans became estranged from God as a result of sin.

We did it our way.

The early Garden of Eden was about partnership with God - but Adam and Eve disobeyed God and as a result brought sin and death upon themselves and their descendants.

We can talk about Adam and Eve bringing physical death, but more significant was the death of relationship with God.

It meant that we had to manage the planet ourselves - with our own wisdom and learning - and we can see the result of this premise in just about every corner of the world.

Adam sinned and from that exact moment, we have all become known to sin.

All have sinned and have fallen short of the glory of God.

And with it we have found ourselves responsible for the consequences.

Look at all the worst things that happen in the world - it is largely attributed to human sin.

Most of diseases and genetic conditions can be put down to human mismanagement, greed, or negligence.

Even global warming.

For those who suffer as a result - they usually see it as unfair, random, unjust.

And we have all felt it and may all feel it at some point in our lives.

Of course, life for human beings is inevitably fatal.

Suffering and death have been synonymous with humanity.

God did not start it this; but should He have stopped it?

He could have; but He did not.

Why?

Jesus uses a similar means of thinking in His parable that sees humanity as tenants in a vineyard - God's vineyard.

When God gave dominion in this world to humanity, they effectively became tenants.

He drew up a tenancy agreement.

In the days when Genesis was written, the verses would have been considered as a sacred covenant.

If they disobeyed, there would be consequences.

Humanity had and has absolute control over all life on the planet to do as they please, how they please.

Being made in the image of God, we are creative, resourceful, and powerful.

And as the landlord, God stepped back.

We have been given free will to exercise control over the Earth.

It started in partnership with God but ended up with the fall.

With us doing our own thing and for humanity there were consequences as promised and that was death.

To Adam He said,

"Because you listened to your wife and ate fruit from the tree about which I commanded you, 'You must not eat from it,' And He said to the man, "You listened to your wife and ate the fruit which I told you not to eat. Because of what you have done, the ground will be under a curse. You will have to work hard all your life to make it produce enough food for you. It will produce weeds and thorns, and you will have to eat wild plants. You will have to work hard and sweat to make the soil produce anything, until you go back to the soil from which you were formed. You were made from soil, and you will become soil again." **Genesis 3:17-19**

We as humanity are responsible for this planet and responsible for those in our community and in this world.

Yes, God is the almighty creator, and He is sovereign over the universe - but He has ceded some of that that responsibility to us as human beings.

And when God makes a covenant - He keeps it.

The tenancy, like all tenancies, will stop one day.

But until then, we have dominion over the Earth.

And the responsibility and consequences of our actions lie firmly at our door.

When we see the suffering in the world today, rather than asking the question,

"Why is God allowing this?"

We should be asking the question "Why are we allowing this?" because most of the suffering in this world right now is preventable.

God does not kill people.

People die.

People kill people.

If someone dies unexpectedly it is not because God has ordained or planned that death.

They have died of whatever they died of - however unfortunate the circumstances - because that is the fate of humanity.

I say this with brevity; but also, with angst and agony.

But my feeling of infirmity will not change the fact

that we all will die, and we do not know when that will be.

In the course of life - we suffer.

All have sinned and fall short of the glory of God.

Is God that 'Cold-Hearted' landlord that just stands by and watch us do this to ourselves?

No!

He is a God of love and does not desire that anyone perish - and He came up with a solution to redeem the world and its unruly tenants.

It is a solution that both answers the question of sin and respects the free will human beings have been given, by providing them a way they might decide to turn back to God.

Any human being who realized that they were trapped in a situation could call out to God.

We have lots of stories in the Old Testament of people who did just that - Noah, Abraham, Isaac, Jacob, etc.

But the perfect expression of God's desire to redeem the world was through the death of Jesus.

God in His grace has always been prepared to forgive sins and went to heroic effort to solve the problem Himself - through Christ.

So, the work of redemption happens one person at a time as people accept and come to experience a true relationship with God for themselves.

And his kingdom extends in that way.

As humans we are responsible to Him for our own sin and as a race for our stewardship of this world.

God will sort out His unruly tenants one day.

Humanity will have to give an account of its awfulness.

"Yet what we suffer now is nothing compared to the glory He will reveal to us later. For all creation is waiting eagerly for that future day when God will reveal who His children really are. Against its will, all creation was subjected to God's curse. But with eager hope, the creation looks forward to the day when it will join God's children in glorious freedom from death and decay. For we know that all creation has been groaning as in the pains of childbirth right up to the present time. And we believers also groan, even though we have the Holy Spirit within us as a foretaste of future glory, for we long for our bodies to be released from sin and suffering." **Romans 8:18-23**

There is a time in the future when God will put right what the dominion of humanity has damaged and destroyed.

Men and women are responsible for their actions and will answer to Him.

But right now, every man and every woman have an opportunity in to turn to Him, find forgiveness and hope and a restored relationship.

To usher in God's work of redemption of His creation.

We extend His kingdom.

And a critical weapon is prayer.

Prayer makes a difference.

We pray:

"Your kingdom come, thy will be done, on earth as it is in heaven."

As God's people we bring that change wherever we are and whoever we are involved with.

Prayer makes a difference - that is a subject itself.

It starts with vibrant prayer.

Because when God's people pray, things really do happen.

Lives are changed; communities transformed.

We can be world changers, and doesn't the world need it?

We are here to alleviate suffering in two ways - by standing for that which is just, right, and free.

But best of all, we can spread, reveal, and minister the word of God.

In doing so, we further God's work of redemption until the day arrives when God fully redeems creation.

And we are the army doing God's purpose of changing minds and hearts - as well as our own, for we have not yet apprehended.

"Trust in the LORD with all your heart and lean not on your own understanding; in all your ways submit to Him, and He will make your paths straight."
<u>Proverbs 3</u>

God never promises us that we will live a life devoid of enduring suffering.

Rather we are told to expect plenty of it in some way or other.

But we are told to do is persevere and trust God as we walk with Him.

As we submit to Him, He makes our paths straight.

Whether they are completely crooked or slightly swayed.

A straight path may mean a miracle - but more often it is about learning to trust God and understanding ourselves and God in ways we had never imagined.

He is a God who can change **NOT ENOUGH** to **MORE THAN ENOUGH** in profound ways.

So, my encouragement to you if you are going through a challenging time, continue to trust in Him, He will carry you through.

I have got to say that what defines us as God's people is not blessed lives.

It is how we find spiritual resources from God in the grimmest times in our lives.

And if we continue to trust, follow, and persevere - we are drawn closer to God and grow in

EXPERIENCE.

EXPERIENCE is **THE MOST VITAL QUALITY** and **THE MOST EFFECTIVE TOOL** in this world today.

Living in the **INFORMATION AGE;** most suck up all their years of education like a sponge and expect to graduate a professional.

In the years to come, in the struggle and situations to come that will try your stability in perplexing situations:

Use these situations to grow in experience.

Some of the most gracious and loving people I have ever met are not the ones blessed with much, but rather those refined in the fire of suffering and that have experienced enough to become **EFFECTIVE.**

Yet what we suffer now is nothing compared to the glory He will reveal to us later.

"For all creation is waiting eagerly for that future day when God will reveal who His children really are."
<u>Romans 8:19</u>

NOTES

Gevind en Verlore

Until we met, I did not know where I was headed.

It was a blind moment as I held the door open one evening and this woman twirled through it.

"Anna Grace," she declared her name and I could feel my cheeks lighting afire before I could glance up.

"Emmanuel," I mumbled, twice because she didn't hear me the first time.

At the time, I was just an eighteen-year-old Special Warfare Combatant Craft Crewmen stationed in Stennis, Mississippi, and she was a twenty-three-old nurse at a children's hospital in Slidell.

I met her as soon as I came back from deployment throughout Saudi Arabia for Counter-Sex-Trafficking operations.

Meanwhile, we were quarantined behind the lonesome register in the convenience store and we began talking when she blatantly asked,

"Where did that come from?" pointing to the scar on my forehead.

"It's a short story with a long explanation," I said with a distraught demeanor.

Without a word, she rolled up her sleeve and revealed a forearm encompassed with shriveling scarred skin.

Before I could glance away, I had already known everything she wanted to tell me, and we were inseparable.

She was talented and remarkably passionate about helping people.

Often more concerned with others wellbeing at the expense of her own.

I, being very secluded and cautious, was not very social to begin with.

Until she came around.

What really tempted me was her touch as I was finally able to speak.

As I spoke of the wounds, she caressed each scar with the palm of her hand.

I shared with her the same things I wrote about.

I never could tell anyone about behind the scenes.

About taking care of my mother when she was sick.

Those nightmares of glass breaking at the farmhouse.

That night I carried my deceased best friend after making a foolish decision.

Watching Chief Warrant Officer Thaddeus Dhatri take his last breath after both of us were shot in the helmet.

Discovering the aftermath of Chief Special Warfare Boat Operator James Morales' suicide after he was told that his wife and daughter were killed in a car accident caused by a drunk driver.

Her face reacted sunken at the jaws with every admitted agonizing memory, but I could tell she was ready to speak something remarkable, something a therapist would prepare to say to an overwhelmed patient.

She reassured me that everything was going to be all right.

But then she told me that I am a 'Good Man'.

Nobody had ever told me that I was a 'Good Man'.

After all the things I have been through and all the things that I have done, I truly did not believe that I could be.

But I felt comfortable believing her.

I had not felt the need to struggle for somebody, but I was willing to endure all things at the price of her seemingly knowledgeable affection.

She always looked at me with captivation.

Her eyes scintillated.

But over time her smile became an illusion as she began to look away with the same intensity.

I doubted everything I had given.

I had wondered if I had either changed her mind or had brought her into captivity, dwelling back on her past the more I unveiled mine.

In a moment of perplexity, I asked if she was happy.

She immediately became hysterical and I just held her.

In a moment of vulnerability, I asked her if she was thinking about somebody else.

"My father... He...."

I just held her.

I had realized that I did not enter the home of a woman simply looking for lost love.

I had waltzed into the catacombs of a world destroyed and abandoned by an abusive father.

The adoptive mother, Victoria, was impotent, and the couple had adopted the two children.

However, the adoptive father, Hadrian, grew sexually, financially, physically, and emotionally abusive.

One night, her father stabbed and killed her mother and then proceeded to blow half of his face off with a shotgun and survive.

Her and her sister were left, once again, to the foster care system and adopted at the age of nine.

I really could not fathom or begin to relate.

I never asked her about anything after that.

But she brought it up every day and kept both of us awake at night re-living the horror as she drank her weight in liquor and wine.

I made it a point to show her that I would stand up

when she called and stand by even when she would rather have nobody there at all, and she would say something like,

"You don't belong with me."

Maybe, but I was happy.

I was committed to be a virgin until marriage, and that soon made our relationship feel like a counseling session.

I always felt there was something that she was keeping from me, and I clearly noticed the prescription bottles stuffed in her nightstand that she rustled through every twenty-minutes, but I feared that she would consider my concern to be overbearing.

I did not want her to feel she has to be perfect to love me.

So, I didn't ask any questions.

We were completely intertwined with each other and couldn't function without one another.

I asked to take her hand in marriage after six months.

I was blinded by love.

Even though I knew all about her past - I really didn't know her at all.

I didn't know her under stress.

I didn't know her temptations.

I didn't know her discouragers.

I didn't know her in bad health.

I didn't know her in poverty.

I didn't know her - but when time past - I came to know a woman that I didn't fall in love with.

A woman that was hateful when she couldn't pay her bills - a woman that was vengeful when she was sick in her own body.

A woman that lost the will to help because she was discouraged by the pains of her past and the anxieties of her future.

She quit her job at the hospital - and she became a chronic alcoholic.

I tried to explain to her how I felt about her drinking and how our relationship was taking a turn for the worst, and that's when things spiraled out of control.

She didn't say anything, she just grabbed a kitchen knife and ran towards me, I didn't know what to do, I almost grabbed her arm, but I remembered those nights at the farmhouse - and I just froze.

I felt like the same little boy getting thrown into the bayou - because this attack wasn't from an enemy - it was from someone I loved.

She sliced my arm and blood started pouring over the carpet, so I grabbed a cloth and wrapped it around the wound before I quickly grabbed my bag and sprinted for the door.

I never looked back.

Had I been there, maybe things would feel different even though there was no changing it.

Many times she threatened to commit suicide, and I always ran back to save her.

She used suicide to control me.

But this time I didn't think she wanted me to save her.

I thought she wanted me gone – for good.

I didn't think twice about her trying to hurt herself, and I was literally running back to base to the clinic in panic because the blood wouldn't stop coming out and I felt like I was going to collapse on the ground.

I made it to the gate and one of the guards literally carried me to the clinic like I was wounded in combat.

I returned to my bunk on base after getting patched up in the clinic and rested that night, hoping the next day she would be sober and willing to talk things out.

I tried to call her the next day when I woke up, but she didn't answer.

I still wasn't afraid, I just thought she wasn't awake yet or maybe she was trying to avoid me.

I took the same twelve mile walk to her apartment, I knocked on the door - she didn't answer.

I tried to open the door - it was locked.

I knew her neighbor, an older woman named Marian, had a spare key because when Anna and I went out of town a few weekends ago, Marian would make sure her plants were watered.

I knocked on Marian's door and asked her to unlock the door for me - and I wish I didn't - I wish she didn't have to see it.

As I opened the door, I could see her feet hanging out of the bedroom.

Marian gasped and ran over before I did - I was still standing in the doorway hoping that she would wake up as Marian shook her in her hands.

I didn't even go inside - I immediately took out my phone called for an ambulance - but then the dispatch woman asked me if she was still breathing - so I walked over and put my hand on her wrist, and I told the dispatcher she was pulseless.

Her skin was cyanotic, her hair was slick, her eyes were whiter than snow - I knew it was too late.

I lost complete control.

I couldn't help but feel as if it were my fault for leaving her alone.

I was completely disheartened.

I felt as if I were being crucified for trying to love someone with all my heart, mind, and soul.

Everything was revoked because of the everlasting love that unconditionally bound my spirit.

However, I do know my love was enough.

She experienced a fatal overdose after drinking half of an entire bottle of vodka and consuming the rest of her bottle of Diazepam.

While at her funeral, her family blamed me for everything that happened and asked me,

"How could you show your face around here? How could you abuse my daughter? How could you treat her like that?"

I kept receiving death threats in text messages and e-mails.

One day during training, we were running rappel drills from an SH-60.

I was not suicidal.

I was overwhelmed.

I closed my eyes and thought about jumping.

My body leaned toward the bliss.

"My heart can take on any form.

A meadow of gazelles,

A cloister of monks,

For the idols, sacred ground,

The same shelter for the pilgrim,

The tables of the Torah,

The scrolls of the Quran.

My creed is love.

Wherever its caravan turns along the way,

That is my belief.

That is my faith."

-Ibn Arabi

Exitium

It is hardest on most comfortable days.

Where the mood is as right as the rain outside of my window.

I still trace droplet paths.

As a child it was the only game I was allowed to play.

As a man it was a hopeless attempt to recall tears of joy.

Only there were none.

A single drop could suppress the flame of a matchstick.

But if these curtains catch a spark.

There is not enough to even begin to delay the perfervid blaze.

And there is nobody coming to save me.

While I am terrified.

Some arsonist finds beauty.

Yet, we both meditate on conflagration.

Respite

Mark 4:35-41

"That day when evening came, He said to His disciples, "Let us go over to the other side." Leaving the crowd behind, they took Him along, just as He was, in the boat. There were also other boats with him. A furious squall came up, and the waves broke over the boat, so that it was nearly swamped. Jesus was in the stern, sleeping on a cushion. The disciples woke Him and said to Him, "Teacher, don't you care if we drown?"

He got up, rebuked the wind and said to the waves, "Quiet! Be still!" Then the wind died down and it was completely calm.

He said to His disciples, "Why are you so afraid? Do you still have no faith?"

They were terrified and asked each other, "Who is this? Even the wind and the waves obey Him!""

In the previous verse - Jesus and his disciples are on a fishing boat in the Sea of Galilee.

Squalls are very much common in the Mediterranean.

And though it does not rain often, there are tremendous bouts of rainfall and ghastly winds that quickly turn the waters into a dangerous place.

The fishermen among Jesus' disciples were aware of

this; but the squall before them had left even the most skilled among them fearing for their lives.

But Jesus was resting, calmly.

Sleeping through the terrors of the disciples and the grave crackles on the structure of the boat from the waterfall downpouring from the clouds above.

His disciples went on to wake him up and ask,

"Don't you even care?"

Eerily similar to the situations, circumstances and storms that cause us to throw up our hands and wonder,

"God, don't you even care?"

How about those living in proximity to conflict?

Syria, Yemen, Burkina Faso, Afghanistan, Libya, Mozambique, **ETC.**

People's lives **AROUND THE WORLD** have been routinely stricken by war and natural disaster.

There are **TOO MANY** areas of the world characterized by injustice, oppression, poverty, prejudice.

How do those that are disadvantaged and powerless escape?

What can they do?

What can we do?

How many people in our own country, our own

community, or our own family feel empathy and agony about things they cannot seem to change?

How many of us wonder where is God?

How many of us wonder what is He doing?

Does God really care about those that have been maimed and killed?

Does He care about the children suffering from malnutrition and that lack health care that are dying from easily curable injuries, illnesses, and diseases?

Does He care that little hope exists around the world?

Does He hear the cries of people struggling?

Is He aware of the injustice, oppression, poverty, and prejudice?

What about my family's problems?

My personal issues?

They seem feverish in comparison, though they are quite common in this world today.

We live in a world that has abandoned God.

Our own society has turned their backs on Him.

And many say if there is a God - why doesn't He care?

In a world where God is rejected, it is not uncommon to find despair and hopelessness.

But today, we find the struggle emerging amongst

younger people.

Teen suicide is the highest it has ever been and rising.

So, does God care?

Looking back on that day of the storm Jesus was on the Sea of Galilee - He was just a passenger.

The experienced sailors were in charge and they were unable to handle the boat.

Interestingly, the person who probably built the boat was in it.

But that night He was not responsible for sailing it - the disciples were.

Our world is God's; He created it.

However, He put us in charge.

We are collectively in charge as Humanity.

What happens is our responsibility.

And we have been managing it for many thousands of years.

When awful things happen, you do not find God at the root.

You find people.

Humans make and use weapons.

Humans rape and murder.

Humans commit crimes.

Humans cause starvation and cause environmental destruction.

We are responsible for it and so, honestly, what are we doing about it as a society and individuals who are part of a rich, powerful democratic country that has power to change things in a positive way?

And when we fail whose fault is it?

Don't we care?

Why haven't we done anything about it?

That day Jesus responded by rising from his slumber, rebuked the wind and said to the waves,

"Quiet! Be still!"

Then the wind died down and it was completely calm.

They did not see that one coming.

So, if the question remains:

"God, don't you care about the sinfulness, the evil, the atrocities, the awfulness of humanity?"

Rest assured that indeed, **HE DOES CARE**.

In fact, He passionately cares; and He has already acted.

Here is what He did:

JOHN 3:16

"For God so loved the world, that He gave his only Son, that whoever believes in Him should not perish

but have eternal life."

Jesus died so that we can find forgiveness for our sins and through that He has also brought those together who trust in God to make that difference in society.

God cares and has raised **US** up to bring that change to humanity.

We are the answer.

God does care and shows it in the many ways that people serve the community wherever they are found through faith.

You may think,

"How can I make a difference? I'm just one person; I'm not significant."

But by each of us making at least an attempt at making a difference, it adds up to a miracle!

And by God's power, think of where that can take us!

NOTES

Who is my neighbor?

Quarantined in this dark room...

I can still hear the nurses in the hallway complaining about whose turn it is to change my dressing.

I woke up getting ready to go home every day, for several months.

Instead I had to have what seemed to be the entire faculty of physicians and nursing students remove a sponge the width and length of a soda can out of my back exposing the delicate nerves of my spine.

If that wasn't torture enough, they had to replace it.

It was so painful that I found myself waiting until the next time they came.

I would clench, curl, flinch and fear waiting until the next time they hurt me.

It was similar to the incidents of complete peril as I gazed in retrospect of my friend's skull being crushed or the sound of my crackling ribs.

Except I could discern that fearing over something that happened in the past is no contender with fearing over something that is imminent and bound to occur in the future.

Immersed in past perils, I couldn't fathom that my brother was having his first child and my mother was diagnosed with breast cancer.

His wife visiting me with a baby-bump and my mother visiting me with her head shaved while I lied on my stomach in agonizing pain and ultimate defeat.

I questioned why God gave me the grace to let it all go.

Why He thought I was worthy of enveloping in a swathe of healing.

Before, I was hindered from being able to love with all my mind, body, and soul.

I lacked the ability to have a cathartic relationship with the issues of life prior to my entire life being turned upside down.

It may have ironically seemed easier to withstand the pressure during the struggle, however, without consistent renewal I inevitably became discouraged.

Self-hatred caused the terrorist to not only attack my body from within but further encouraged the attack to unleash against the people in my life, especially those whom I loved most.

But that was my release.

I didn't have a way to relieve or even communicate the pressure and I began abusing my way out.

Whoever showed the most affection received the worst reaction.

But when nobody said anything at all, there was a deduction from my character.

Silence curded my perspective into a distasteful, agonizing and completely incorrect one.

I could no longer live like that.

So, what I did is I prayed.

Without a church raising me.

Without a ministry or a college to teach me.

I never even cracked open a bible.

But, even just as I simply prayed, I found a release.

When I prayed, I found a place and a person that saw what I did, understood my thoughts and temptations but knew I was ready when He heard my cry shouting from the bottom of a pit to the heavenlies that claimed the suffering and the sacrifice as tribute for every day I took for granted and for every curse I delivered through my mouth and my own two hands.

By having a cathartic relationship with God, I remained open to great affection and successes but also vulnerable to devastating hurts and insurmountable disappointments.

I grew the capacity to overcome my adversities along with the capacity to obtain and maintain the blessings He had in store for me.

The relief of having a cathartic relationship with God is having the ability to have devoted relationships with the individuals that come to cross my path and having the grace to touch the lives of people who are normally mocked and beaten, most times by the people I idolize and have an innate responsibility to stand by.

This continuous attack has played a key role in instilling the values from my own heart into the people near and dear to me when I choose to sacrifice their suggestions of bigotry and bias to throw my hand out for the same people they ridicule and slander.

My love affair with God was more palatable as it simultaneously cleansed my spirit and influenced those around me.

Despite my perspective of my own demise, and despite others understanding, I continued to expect to wake up one day by the side of the woman I love, having my wounds stitched and scars held and allow me to feel what I have aspired to do for not only them, but for others as well.

To be loved unconditionally as I have even the strangest of strangers.

As I delved into the word of God, I even found reasons to start looking but kept waiting in fear of a successful relationship as much as a failing one.

As a result of my incompetence I was left without any revelation or sight of who I was looking for.

Nevertheless, I believe that when I come to lay my restless eyes on who God has in store for me that I will know without any doubt and be able to fall into safe love and spend my latter days in the comfort of a stable commitment and vibrant connection that could still stand firm if the presence of pure happiness was to become diminished.

My cry intertwined with the wind and convinced the soil that anything that grows from this must surely be fruit-bearing and bring something to sustain me.

There could be no limit on my love.

My garden has grown much since I planted that first seed and decided to grow with God and become a conduit to heal other hurting people all around this world.

Although, I have always seemed to attach most sufficiently to those that have been dismissed, much like myself.

Those that have endured part-time love and fulltime despair.

An extended period of trouble in a brief period of time.

It is more of a purpose than a fetish to wish to bring to others what you wish to bring to yourself with only the intention of loving them gracefully, not with fickleness, frailness, and fornication.

Indeed, it is exciting to know that somebody will never forget you because you loved them without taking, breaking, or turning around and expecting something specific in return.

To endure and sacrifice rather than burden and condemn.

Whatever the case may be, I draw great courage,

strength, tenacity, pertinacity and understanding rather than simple pleasure from my experiences and I am forever content knowing that all I did and ever could do healed somebody in need of a touch from God and aided me on my journey to become the best type of person I can offer the world.

The salt upon my wounds further discerned my neighbors.

My neighbors are those who are misfits and misunderstood.

Which surely is every man and woman on this planet.

Knowing that I am not alone has saved me, bandaged my wounds, and caressed my scars.

And finding the ability to love myself with my whole mind, my whole body and my whole spirit is just as much of a blessing as finding the love of my eternity.

If I could know of a greater love than the love of God, then I would not even embark to fathom the mystery.

This is enough.

His grace is sufficient.

"Give light and people will find a way."

-Ella Baker

Deditio

I surrender.

My life is not my own.

I surrender.

To you I belong.

I surrender.

The breath in my lungs is at your mercy.

I surrender.

The bones in my body orchestrate at your will.

I surrender.

Amalgamation

Broken World.

That is a term we tend to come across frequently these days, don't we?

We do not have to listen exceptionally long to the radio, watch the television, or read in a post on social media that we live in a very troubled world.

The war in Syria - the activities of ISIS - the Taliban - Paris - London - Boko Haram in Nigeria - ETC.

These all reflect the horrors of, indeed, a Broken World.

We cannot fail to miss many of the ills of our own society reflected in our own communities and neighborhoods.

And to be fair, it always was.

Some of the current troubled parts of the world have always been troubled.

For that matter, our own nation has a history of the injustice, war and all the rest of it.

Recalling the start of World War One - it was termed 'The Great War' because it was expected to be the war that was to end all wars and restore order to the world.

Though, more bodies have been claimed and blood have been shed in the name of war since then; and is it really so far away?

My friend's great-grandmother was slave.

That is merely a few generations from oppression.

And many dismiss the pains spoken from children and grandchildren in this day; they tell them not to think about it or dwell on it because it is a thing of the past; but the idols still stand.

The statues which symbolize discrimination and division still radiate, shamelessly.

Look back through all of history, and all the wars to come had the same story.

Plenty examples of a Broken World.

Why is our World so Broken?

The humanists, sociologists, politicians, philosophers and even the cashier at the super-market will all give you their opinion on this subject.

But the Bible gives us answers - and it goes right back to the root of our faith:

"When Adam sinned, sin entered the world. Adam's sin brought death, so death spread to everyone, for everyone sinned."

Humanity has rebelled against God and it goes right back to the start.

"When Adam sinned, sin entered the world."

Right from the start of humanity, from the very first people, everyone has rebelled against God.

"Yes, people sinned even before the law was given. But it was not counted as sin because there was not yet any law to break. Still, everyone died - from the time of Adam to the time of Moses - even those who did not disobey an explicit commandment of God, as Adam did."

This gave an answer to those that said,

"How can God judge and condemn people if they don't have access to His Law?"

Well, for the same reason that in the absence of a set of instructions, you still know something is wrong.

So, people before Moses and the Law did that which was wrong.

We saw evidence of that in their societies and actions.

Their World was as Broken as ours.

They knew instinctively what was right and wrong and did wrong.

But the Law was like the command to Adam.

When Adam and Eve sinned, they committed a willful violation of a direct command from God.

That was direct rebellion against Him.

There are those who know right and wrong as God defines it because we have the Ten Commandments.

But people still know and understand right and wrong even though there is not a sign saying, '*HIGH VOLTAGE*'.

All have sinned and come short of God's glory.

I find few optimists in the world today.

There used to be those in the philosophical and even theological communities who thought that by education, science, and reasoning that the world would be civilize.

But their numbers have diminished over the years.

Where you do find them, they invariably blame everything they declare irrational - including religion - for the world's faults.

What we find in scriptures is a simpler, but more lachrymose prognosis of our Broken World.

When we understand what Paul is trying to tell us in **Romans 5**, then we understand that how it has been is what it is going to continue to be the case until God, as prophesied calls a stop to it when Jesus returns.

It will never get better until then.

But that is the whole point of **Romans 5**.

It is part of a whole section of Romans that tells us that God has already taken action to deal with the issue of human sin in order to restore our relationship with Him.

Just as in Adam - all have sinned.

Now in Jesus all can find life and hope.

Adam is a symbol - a representation of Christ, who was yet to come.

"But there is a significant difference between Adam's sin and God's gracious gift."

What are those differences?

We are told three things.

1.) CHRIST BRINGS FORGIVENESS

"For the sin of this one man, Adam, brought death to many. But even greater is God's wonderful grace and His gift of forgiveness to many through this other man, Jesus Christ."

Adam brought death to humanity and we see that death all around us.

Not just in physical death, but also in the death of relationships, the death of forgiveness, the death of selflessness, the death of love, and all the rest of what is honorable and compassionate in this world.

But Jesus brings us back into relationship with God.

God in His grace - in His unmerited favor - sent His own Son into the world to die for us.

It is through Him in which each person can find forgiveness.

Paul calls God's sacrifice the gift of forgiveness.

He seeks no reparation in return.

He brings forgiveness.

2.) CHRIST BRINGS RELATIONSHIP WITH GOD

"And the result of God's gracious gift is quite different from the result of that one man's sin. For Adam's sin led to condemnation, but God's gift leads to our being made right with God, even though we are guilty of many sins."

Along with forgiveness comes a restoration of our relationship that was lost by Adam.

With sin came condemnation - but through Christ we are made right with God despite of who we are.

Jesus brings us into relationship with Him.

We do not have to go much further in Romans or in other parts of the New Testament to see all the blessings that God pours out on those who trust and follow Jesus.

3.) CHRIST BRINGS US HOPE

Those of us who are faithful have a hope that should change our lives.

No longer do we have to live with sin but live in triumph over it.

We saw how we were called not to live according to the elementary principles of the world.

We have figuratively died to childish things.

They are all part of Adam.

We are now able to live in triumph over sin and death through Christ Jesus.

So why don't we?

The message we bring is a message of hope to a World that is Broken by sin, following the way of Adam.

But can we make a difference?

It looks ominous and discouraging - but, certainly, absolutely, and without a doubt.

How?

"One-man disobeyed God, many became sinners. But because one other person obeyed God, many will be made righteous."

How do people get to understand how they are made righteous?

Because God has a way of communicating that information to them.

You know who that is.

You and me.

Can it make a difference to others?

You know the answer to that too because once it made a difference to you.

Further faith is growing fast in many parts of the world - despite denomination - and it is <u>ALL</u> for the love of <u>OUR</u> God.

We also know that in this country, and many others, that there have been massive spurts of growth from time to time.

And that occurs when God's people realize just who

they are in Him, realize just what sort of God we serve, and commit ourselves in the Spirit to pray, call, and hope for the power of God to come and change our country and our situation.

It does happen - but we need to be a people who are committed, watchful, prayerful, and persevering for it.

We are outposts of God's Kingdom, bringing its values to a Broken World.

But there is more to this than just seeing personal revival.

Because our experience is that when the Church of God mobilizes, it can be positive change and lead to transformations in society.

We are called to be a transforming people.

We have already been made citizens of another place.

We are already in God's Kingdom, or rather His Kingdom rests inside of Us.

"He loves us, and by His sacrificial death He has freed us from our sins and made us a kingdom of priests to serve His God and Father." <u>Revelations 1:5</u>

This premise is further amplified by something Jesus says in Luke's gospel.

"Some Pharisees asked Jesus when the Kingdom of God would come. His answer was, "The Kingdom of God does not come in such a way as to be seen. No one will say, "Look, here it is!' or, "There it is!';

because the Kingdom of God is within you.""<u>Luke 17:20-21</u>

The Kingdom of God is in all of our hearts.

The Kingdom of God is not about territory, but about allegiance.

Even in the darkness of a Broken World, the Kingdom of God is being extended.

And we are called to be tenacious as we strive to grow, spread, and extend it here.

Each time there are huge movements of the Spirit, there are transformations in society associated with it.

But as in all situations like this - if this change is to be sustained and remain consistent from generation to generation, then we need to keep reaching forward and throwing our blessings on future generations.

The decline in the church and in the influence in our society is because, for whatever reason, we have not reached the upcoming generation as the previous one left.

And we are called to reach out to our corner of this Broken World and ensure that the future brings healing and peace.

We need to dedicate ourselves to it, because when God's people commit, things really do happen.

The situation really changes.

And maybe one day, we may witness the evolution from a World that is Broken into a World that is

Whole.

I will continue to pray for that because I believe it is not only possible, but that a breakthrough is imminent and will lead from God's word to the evolution of mankind.

<u>NOTES</u>

Discouraged

When I came home after sitting in the hospital for nearly two months, I found myself depressed, lonely, and sexually frustrated.

I had spent my nights and days cuddling my pillow like it was Anna and crying myself to sleep.

When I closed my eyes, I could imagine her head laying on my chest and her arms limply wrapped around my body as she slumbered peacefully.

I could no longer go on hikes anymore because her silhouette met me at the top of the mountain.

The big, strong, courageous man I used to be was gone – with her.

Soon, I was at the bar looking for a woman to take home so that I could pretend it was her.

But when I finally brought one home, I panicked when she touched me.

She didn't make me feel as comfortable as her.

I told her a thousand times we could go back to my place and just watch movies, talk, and order food – I was not interested in having sex with someone I just met – nor even before marriage.

She didn't hold my hand or react with emotion to the things I said, just a nod and a shrug of the shoulders – and she wasn't willing to go on a date or be in a relationship with a man whom is saving himself for marriage – she just wanted to have sex.

I tried to talk about taking care of my mother when she was sick – she nodded.

Those nightmares of glass breaking at the farmhouse – she shrugged her shoulders.

That night I carried my deceased best friend after making a foolish decision – she looked at me as if I had two heads.

Watching Chief Warrant Officer Thaddeus Dhatri take his last breath after both of us were shot in the helmet – she looked at my scar in disgust rather than in awe of the tragedy at hand.

Discovering the aftermath of Chief Special Warfare Boat Operator James Morales' suicide after he was told that his wife and daughter were killed in a car accident caused by a drunk driver – she stood up and left.

I realized that I couldn't bring just anybody back home.

I couldn't let just anyone hear the burdens on my heart either – I had to be selectively permeable.

I felt like I was allowing myself to give up on a loving relationship because of my temptation towards Anna – because she was gone, and I didn't have anywhere else to release these emotions.

But I came to understand that my temptation for Anna wouldn't go away after laying with this random woman I just met at the bar.

Not that easily.

Could I somehow be with her again?

Could I find someone like her?

Could someone that sees me like she saw me?

She told me many times that I was a 'Good Man".

She spoke countless compliments and showered me with praise as if I didn't have any sin or infidelities in my life.

She healed my anxieties and insecurities with her compassionate and unscripted words.

Where could I find this love again?

I decided to give up.

I figured it wasn't worth it - the search would be never ending.

I would never find abounding and true love again.

I would be broken and ashamed for the rest of my life.

For some odd reason, I found no other direction but to turn to God.

He was all that I had left - and He has never failed me.

I decided I would give my life to God and let him use me to be an answer rather than bring another complaint.

To be a solution rather than a problem that needs

solving.

Maybe if I turn to Him – I could help another man or woman in the same position.

Would that make me feel better?

If I could just give the same love that I gave Anna to people hurting just like me – will I find a breakthrough?

If I could show them that I am sincere and that my love is luxurious and unbound.

That even though I have been buried - my love for the world and the infatuation that God has constantly revealed to me even when I felt unworthy has brought me from the grave.

Hastening towards this life that I had a vision to create despite the sound of embers crackling in the wind, the sight of fire engrossing everything I have ever loved, and the smell of smoke stained in my nostrils.

My prayer to myself is to stay consistent.

To stay committed to the call on my life.

To be a loving man in spite of all the hate and negativity in this world.

To lay my head to rest only when I am sure that this deed is done.

To fight these principalities until my very last breath.

I do not know where I will end up on this mission – but I know where to begin.

I have always wished I had some type of medical training - maybe I could have saved them – or her.

Then again, maybe not.

While I was praying one night – I had the most intense flashback.

The Chinook used to carry our SOC-R was hit by an RPG.

I watched the helicopter split in half and as we began to fall, I blacked out.

When I woke up, I found myself buried under a mountain of equipment.

My first thought:

"I am alive."

My second thought:

"I can't breathe."

I forced out a lungful of air, spitting out most of my teeth along with a desperate breath.

Lost teeth were the least of my worries.

With the crash's flames bearing down, I threw off the equipment that had me pinned.

I soon realized that part of what I had to remove wasn't just equipment - it was body parts.

I didn't have time to consider the gruesome scene.

The heat inside the helicopter cooked off round after round of ammunition - which began to pop and crack.

I crumpled to the ground when I tried to stand.

It was crawl or die.

I dragged myself toward the screams of those outside who were begging for the rest to escape.

When I looked to my right, the pilot was laying on the ground, clutching a hole in her throat.

When I looked to my left, Chief Warrant Officer Dhatri was staring at me with a hole in his head, and I watched as his brown eyes turned into glass and his skin turned cyanotic before I could even think.

The pilot screeched and she gulped for air.

Dhatri was gone.

Bullets were still whizzing by my head from the ammunition being cooked off inside the helicopter.

I didn't see the explosion.

I only felt it as the heat engulfed my back.

For a few moments I couldn't hear anything.

Then the only things I could hear were screams.

When I looked up, the fire brightened the night sky and the wreckage below.

The pilot was holding onto my shoulder with one hand - the other hand was trying to control the blood pouring from her neck.

I took both hands and tried to stop the bleeding, but

nothing helped.

I kept telling her,

"It will be okay! It will be okay!"

I don't know why; I didn't even believe it.

I just did.

I was stuck holding her neck - my legs were broken; I couldn't walk and I could feel my helmet indenting an imprint into my skull.

The damage was done.

We weren't doctors.

And even if we had been, it wouldn't have mattered.

Most of them were dead even before we hit the ground.

"I've learned that people will forget what you said, People will forget what you did, But people will never forget how you made them feel."

-Maya Angelou

Indebted

There is something about struggle.

It brings out the worst in the best of us.

And the best in the worst of us.

I wonder if I was strong enough before.

Or if God tried me by fire because He knew something I didn't.

Would I have made it before?

Would I have had this intensity?

Would I have helped others?

Or just helped me?

Maybe it is better not to know at all.

But I am grateful.

I am still melancholic over the past.

But I am grateful.

Seclusion

It seems obvious that the effects of loneliness and social isolation are detrimental to physical, emotional, and spiritual health.

But do we really understand the magnitude of this issue?

Many adults and even children experience loneliness and social isolation.

Many of us reading this right now have experienced or know someone who has experienced significant loneliness.

With the use of technology increasing both at home and in the workplace, maybe this is not such a surprise.

We now have the ability to choose virtual relationships over physical almost without exception.

We are disconnecting from real relationships and are instead spending more time alone, which results in feeling less rested and more stressed.

Go anywhere in public and you will find people with faces buried in their cell phones or fingers typing vigorously on their laptops.

Now, technology is an all-encompassing evil.

There are many redeeming qualities: it allows families and friends to connect across borders, stay-at-home parents to earn an income while caring for children and increases efficiency amongst industries.

It also allows many of us that do not have access to ministry as readily as others directly on the internet through online sermon videos and blogs.

However, we have a challenging time unplugging ourselves from technology, feeling like in doing so we might miss out on something.

It seems what we are really missing out on is being truly present with one another.

So how can we as a community decrease this experience of loneliness and social isolation?

How can we be more intentional and vulnerable in our relationships?

Maybe it starts with having lunch with a friend or looking our loved ones in the eyes and giving them space to express their feelings fully with someone who cares to listen wholeheartedly.

How can we increase our own social interactions and combat this mentality?

I think it is important to remind ourselves of how many around us are experiencing loneliness and social isolation.

Would we be more conscious of this and share the love of Christ with others?

All it takes is a kind word, simple gesture, or act of service.

Write a card, offer to pray, lift someone up with

encouragement.

As we reflect on the meaning of love, would we be reminded of the true love of Christ; the perfect love of the Father who laid down the life of His own Son so that we would feel the depth of His care and concern for us, His children?

Through God we are welcomed into a holy family, joined with our brothers and sisters, and invited into a joy filled eternity with our Lord.

As we ponder what it means to love one another, shall we meditate on these words from Scripture that encourage us to reach out and share God's love with those who are feeling isolated and lonely?

Shall we be the hands and feet of Jesus, sharing the message of His love in the workplace, in our friendships, our homes, our communities, and our world?

Not just when it is convenient, but every day and every time we have the opportunity.

"A new commandment I give to you, that you love one another: just as I have loved you, you also are to love one another. By this all people will know that you are my disciples, if you have love for one another." __John 13:34-35__

"So then you are no longer strangers and aliens, but you are fellow citizens with the saints and members of the household of God, built on the foundation of the apostles and prophets, Christ Jesus Himself being the cornerstone, in whom the whole structure,

being joined together, grows into a holy temple in the Lord. In Him you also are being built together into a dwelling place for God by the Spirit."Ephesians 2:19-22

"And let us consider how to stir up one another to love and good works, not neglecting to meet together, as is the habit of some, but encouraging one another, and all the more as you see the Day drawing near."Hebrews 10:24-25

"This is how we know what love is: Jesus Christ laid down His life for us. And we ought to lay down our lives for our brothers and sisters."1 John 3:16

NOTES

Resurrected by Love

I prayed for a career that could put me in a position to reach out and heal people.

To pay respect to my fallen squad mates – to make peace with the fact that I left Anna to die.

That is when I decided to become a Paramedic.

I was sitting there in my room and I was praying to be an answer to someone's prayer during a desperate time.

To be a comforter in someone's time of need for intervention, whether life-saving or spiritual.

And so, I started Paramedic school with the notion that I would be giving myself away so that God can use me.

So that God can utilize me.

On my weekends off from school, I worked Friday through Sunday at a Respite Care facility taking care of intellectually and developmentally disable children.

They helped calm my Post Traumatic Stress Disorder and I learned more about being a compassionate caregiver than I ever did while working in the hospital or on the ambulance.

Incidentally, when I can home every night from school and work, I wrote in countless notebooks and filled the pages with my heart and soul to convey a message of spiritual healing to no one but myself.

With my mother's diagnosis of stage 3 metastatic breast cancer, I was motivated to learn new things that I could go home and use to help her.

Whether it was simply taking her blood pressure, changing her bandages, or draining her surgical drains following her double mastectomy.

I really didn't see myself as mature enough to handle it, intellectual enough to pass through all of the tests, or strong enough to break through all the obstacles - but I was fortified through the thought that I would one day be an answer to somebody's prayer- my own or someone else's mother, child, or family members prayer when they are in desperate need of someone relentless and resilient enough to stand the sight of the things I would come to see, and also caring and compassionate.

Coming home and hearing her weary voice as she laid there in pain put a lump in my throat that I carried with me.

It is not as though I was born to work as a Paramedic - I was successful simply because it has always been God's purpose in my life for me to be a solution and a comforter- and it has always been my will to act on it and work towards being that kind of person despite my own despair.

Despite the pain and the feeling of inequity.

Being there for my own and other countless families in need during desperate times of sickness or tragedy lit a fire in my heart that since has made me genuinely care for others and appreciate life despite past circumstances and my own stresses.

Being the one that others looked to made me swallow my pride and work tirelessly with humility to provide what they needed- whether it was being a son to my mother, a life-saving intervention, a home for the weekend while families dealt with bereavement, or a simple dialogue to put patients at ease.

It didn't make me forget, but it made me grateful to still be alive myself.

It makes me feel like an answer to a problem and like I am doing the work that God put me on this Earth to do, especially in a world where many of us really don't know what to do, or where to go and often feel like we are not enough.

There is nothing I have ever gone through, nothing that I have ever seen, done, or heard of that would make me question whether God can use you.

And with that, I pray no matter what we all endure that we grow better & not bitter!

I still ask Him to correct my attitude and my consistency at times, but I have never stopped believing that I could become those things which He called me to be!

I believe that I am an effective Paramedic - but more importantly - A Man of Faith Next Door, without questioning my ability to stand in the capacity in which I am called.

And I surrender all that I am so that God can use me to be a light in the darkness.

However, I soon found myself overwhelmed as I was working for a cause and a purpose much bigger than myself.

I kept bringing home the pain of my work.

The patients that stuck with me was a three-month old child that took her last breath in my arms, and her mother and father wept on each side of me.

An elderly man whose closed curtains had gone unnoticed by his busy neighbors while he laid decomposing into his own carpet.

A man whose brains covered my gloves hand as my colleague, and I lifted his limp and bloody body into a bag after he murdered his wife in front of their child and then shot himself in the face.

A small, wafer thin, dead child curled up on his Toy Story duvet after drinking his parents' medication that they use to help with their addictions.

And the worst of all – two little girls.

These little girls were covered in sores that were filled with maggots.

Naked and laying in their own excrement.

The room we found them in was completely bare – expect for three bottles of solid-sour milk.

And a tripod camera.

I approached the bigger one – my partner, a female,

approached the younger.

As I walked towards her, they both screamed helplessly, and we didn't know why.

And then a cop walked in carrying a massive box of video tapes.

We look at the tripod.

These little girls are terrified of men – and now we know why.

My partner picks up both of the little girls and is carrying them in her arms – still naked and filled with excrement – I told her to wait while I ran to the back of the ambulance to grab towels to wrap them with.

The whole ride to the hospital, these little girls clung to my partner and would not let go.

When we arrived at the ER, they still wouldn't let go so my partner held them while they drew their blood for labs – they didn't even flinch.

Finally, they sedated them so that they could complete the exam, but until they fell asleep – they still clung to my partner and would not let go.

Maggots dropped onto the floor as she laid them down on the hospital bed.

When the labs came back – they both had Gonorrhea and Herpes of the mouth and genitalia.

They were emaciated, dehydrated, and sick.

Their hair was shorn and matted.

The younger girl had brain damage.

My heart wasn't just broken – it was ripped out of my chest and thrown into a furnace.

I was crying, my partner was crying, the nurses and the doctors were crying, the police officers were crying – everybody was crying.

I honestly didn't see myself as worthy of being in this position, I was still very much new to the profession and a student trying to learn all that I could about the job.

I felt filthy, dirty, foolish, and moronic - yet God kept calling me to do this – my heart may have been completely shattered, but I still needed to stand – those little girls couldn't protect themselves.

What if this happens again?

Is this happening somewhere right now?

I felt broken and desperate for the love of God, so I ran to the closest church.

And fate unfolded.

That is where I met her.

I walked in and she took me by the hand while I was crying out to God and she prayed for me.

I told her what had brought me to my knees.

We prayed for those little girls – she had one of her own.

We cried together.

And over the next few months, we fell in love with each other.

We were rooted in the love of God.

The foundation of our love was a prayer asking God to take this mind and spirit away from both of us so that we could live a life of love and abolish all the negative energy.

It was something I truly needed and something I just happened to stumble upon.

Although, I was committed to be a virgin until marriage – and she was not.

She was already married once before to an abusive husband that was impotent and couldn't bear children – she gave birth to her daughter at the age of seventeen and met this man a few years later.

However, I personally never judged a woman for not saving herself.

It was my option to save myself.

I didn't want to be a womanizer or lay with every woman that threw herself at me.

I didn't want to take advantage or exploit a woman's weaknesses for my pleasure.

I will admit that even after we found this captivating towards one another, we both had our times of weakness – I am just grateful that we both allowed ourselves the time to search for answers TOGETHER.

There were times where I walked out the door, and so had she.

I had realized that there was a reason I could not 'win' her immediately.

There was a reason nothing I did could please her - without having sex.

And there was a reason she could not accept me at first for the kind of shy love that I brought to the table.

One day, the woman once fighting against my shy love came to seek it.

After years of feeling like neither of us deserved to be loved - we found that we could love each other.

We could trust each other.

I was comfortable loving her, and she was comfortable loving me.

Even after all that had happened, we felt safe to love because we were always honest and communicated.

We realized that the only problem holding us back from being together was an anxious mind - a fear that things will not work out in the end - a fear that things will turn out the same as they did before in past relationships.

The problem was we both were not allowing ourselves to be loved and to be happy.

And I personally came to the understanding that one must be HEALED enough and feel SAFE enough to let people in that were scared to let you in at first – if you truly want to be loved the way you dream about.

You cannot push people away just because you have an idea of how love is supposed to look – and you can't deny someone from experiencing all of your love just because you're scared.

It takes the luxury out of it and makes it seem like a job.

In this world we are living in, we need to stop pushing the love out of our life just because it is not how we planned it would be – as if anything in our lives has ever went as planned.

And you have got to know who you are well enough to be ready to receive them.

And also understand that if things don't work out, it is simply because God willed it that way.

Not because you are not good enough or because you are unlovable.

And if you choose to love someone that doesn't stay for one reason or another, and you find yourself unacceptable to someone in the future because of the way you lived in the past, then it is because God intended it to be that way also.

They don't deserve you if they can't accept you.

So, don't be afraid to love – as I always have.

The one thing that stayed consistent is that we never held anything against one another, and we always ended up needing each other at the end of each and every day.

We both understand that we will always go through times of uncertainty and even temptation, but we believe that when your relationship has a foundation of prayer and is rooted in the love of God, nothing can come between your connection to one another.

That is something we both agree on – even when we can't agree on a place to eat or when we disagree about who we should vote for in the next election.

Knowing the type of man I am, she motivated me to re-enlist into the military so that I could use my testimony to combat post-traumatic stress disorder and the anxieties faced by men and women that serve our country and communities – and to teach others emergency medical care so that they never have to feel how I felt.

And that is when I knew I chose the right woman to love again.

"Books can capture injustices in a way that stays with you and makes you want to do something about them. That is why they are so powerful."

-Malala Yousafzai

Mom, where do weddings come from?

Love is like a seed.

Not to be buried, but watered.

It will grow if the conditions are in order.

Circumstances change, and with it sometimes people.

But true and honest love stands firm.

It is a virtue.

Not a flickering emotion.

And if you question it, then it was never real.

Real love is unquestionable.

It leaves no room for uncertainty.

No place for inequity to dwell.

And leaves no marks but a smile of satisfaction.

Ruina

"Power tends to corrupt, and absolute power corrupts absolutely. Great men are almost always bad men..."

You are probably familiar with these words, but not the British aristocrat they came from, John Dalberg-Acton.

Simplified, the greater the power, the greater the potential for corruption.

But are all great men bad men?

Is that a sweeping stereotype?

Go through all the greats of world history, male or female, and you will have to work hard to find people of high integrity.

Mao Zedong, for example, attributed political power as always going to be achieved by force.

Hitler once said,

"The bigger the lie, the more likely people will believe it."

Here is a final comment from the worldly wise - or not so wise - if you remember the French philosopher Voltaire.

"To learn who rules over you, simply find out who you are not allowed to criticize."

Fortunate to be in a free country?

That is something you and I can discuss over coffee!

We are fortunate that we live in a free country.

I am also fortunate that many have paved the way and played a pivotal role in establishing many of the freedoms we enjoy.

But beware; guard them jealously because there are those who would take them from us.

Even in societies like the US where there is a strong influence, there is pressure to adopt and practice values that I would deem an attack on basic human rights.

Why am I saying this?

Not so I can give you a politics lesson, because many of you are better read in politics than me.

It is to give you the contrast in the way that God exercises power in comparison to humanity and nothing better typifies this than the triumphal entry into Jerusalem.

Here we see Jesus entering Jerusalem.

Every symbol used that day is the opposite of that a worldly ruler would do in the exercise of his power.

Jesus came on a humble beast of burden, a donkey.

His followers were armed with palm branches, not weapons, which traditionally were symbols of goodness, well-being, and victory.

A king would have carpets spread before him (the red-carpet treatment) as a sign of welcome and obedience.

There was no red carpet for Jesus, so his disciples threw their coats down instead.

And they cried Hosanna.

But it ended up being one man on a donkey.

"The disciples came to Jesus and asked, "Who, then, is the greatest in the kingdom of heaven?" He called a little child and placed the child among them. And He said: "Truly I tell you, unless you change and become like little children, you will never enter the kingdom of heaven."

In Jesus' kingdom, the highest value is humility, putting the needs of others first, caring for the most powerless, and exercising forgiveness.

In fact, everything that is the reverse of human power.

In fact, what the Gospel has done for 2,000 years has challenged and transformed human notions of power and integrity.

The triumphal entry into Jerusalem, preceded the ultimate battle that Jesus would undertake to complete his work on Earth.

Now if he were an earthy leader, he would command a great army so that he could propagate his philosophy and force all the people he conquered to follow him.

The interesting thing about human nations is that they are exclusive clubs.

Not so in the kingdom of God.

It is not exclusive; it's inclusive and it's open to all who would like to become citizens Jesus died so that every man and every woman may have the option of trusting and following Jesus and becoming part of that kingdom.

There is no bureaucracy or hurdles to jump.

He calls all to recognize their sin, their need of forgiveness and to ask God for citizenship.

It is a low hurdle, but it is surprising how many people do not want to jump it!

How about you?

So, what is God's kingdom like.

I would sum it up in three statements of Jesus:

1.) "My kingdom is not of this world." <u>John 18:36</u>

There is a sense that God's kingdom is here because people are invited to join it here.

More on that in a moment.

But the promises of Jesus extend beyond life and into eternity.

God's kingdom is a future event as well as a present reality.

2.) "The kingdom of God is among you." <u>Luke</u>

<u>17:21</u>

Human kingdoms are about territory.

Look at the Syrian War.

It is not just about ideology, religion, or freedom – it all involves the taking or holding of territory.

But the kingdom of God has no territory here.

In the past some have tried to establish territory of behalf of God, like the holy Roman Empire.

Arguably, although human beings like their territories, God is Creator and things ultimately belong to Him anyway.

The reality is that the kingdom of God is about allegiance not territory.

ISIS took territory in Iraq and Syria but what we know from liberated areas, the locals never really followed them and lived in fear of their lives.

Jesus' kingdom is not about territory, but about hearts and minds set on following Him.

3.) "Truly, truly, I say to you, unless one is born again, he cannot see the kingdom of God."<u>John 3:3</u>

The last verse is the most important.

The main way in which most of us got to be American is that we were born here.

We enter the kingdom of God also by birth, what Jesus calls the second birth.

That is a lot less complicated than human birth: it is by simply trusting Jesus and following Him.

If you don't know Jesus already, the offer to follow Him is open to you today.

Are you going to follow Him?

Iter Usque Ad Ultimum Terrae

Re-enlisting into the military wasn't really an option since I had previously attempted to commit suicide.

It was just something that I was born to do - and I felt that I was needed.

I found myself in a world of thought – and then one day I just thought about re-enlisting as a Chaplains Assistant – and I never looked further.

Of course, this was not going to be a precedented process.

The biggest obstacle was providing paperwork from my psychiatrist saying that I was cleared to join back into the service.

This wasn't easy at all, but he told me if I could graduate Paramedic school and continue volunteering at my church and show him that I was strong enough to combat the spirit of post-traumatic stress disorder and depression in men and women working in Emergency Services, he would be willing to sign off.

It took me almost six years to prove that I was motivated to keep living without going back into that mindset and that I was committed to this purpose that I had conjured up.

But I finally did it – and by that time I had not only

completed Paramedic school, but I also received my Master of Divinity Degree.

I cried before he even signed the paper.

When he looked me in my eyes and told me he was amazed that a man could find the strength to fight again, after all that I had been through.

That it is a miracle.

That I am a miracle.

I would walk out of that room a man on a mission for the rest of my life.

I began my journey as a Chaplains Assistant.

Helping orchestrate religious activities and preparing for the services provided by Colonel Powell.

I was asked to preach many times and give my testimony, and that is when I knew that I was molded to be a Chaplain myself.

Even as an assistant, I found myself counseling soldiers and families in need of spiritual guidance because of my experiences in life.

I was providing ministry, support, & comfort to families during bereavement when I was as young as twenty-seven years old.

Some commented on the fact that I was too young and handsome, but I was proven to be effective.

When I finally became a Chaplain, I made a few inquiries that were very personal to me and went to the homes of families of some of the men that I had served with.

I visited Chief Warrant Officer Dhatri's widow and his two daughters.

I was welcomed into the home before I even had the chance to introduce who I really was, and I immediately noticed the pictures of Dhatri and his family that were on each and every wall and decorating the mantle above the fireplace next to his tri-folded burial flag and slew of medals.

I sat down and she brought me a cup of coffee and she asked me what I was there for.

Before I could say anything – I just started crying.

I couldn't bring myself to speak, so I just pointed to the scar on my head, and she knew that it was me who had wrote to her years ago after the incident and she started crying with me.

When I had no more tears left, I finally told her exactly what happened.

Although it was a tragic revelation, it seemed to bring her a sense of relief.

Rather than hear it from someone who was there to deliver a message and do their job, it came from a man that was a brother to her husband and served right beside him.

I told her about all of our tours and all of our accomplishments.

Some of our most memorable were missions we were not even supposed to be involved with.

Our squad was sent to Accra after heavy rainfall flooded the largest city in Ghana, and as waters receded, we started hauling deceased on dump trucks.

We were sent to Japan after the Kumamoto earthquakes to evacuate hospitals and transport newborns in their incubators.

We were also sent to the Northern Mariana Islands after a category five typhoon wiped out entire communities, and we rummaged through remnants of capsized homes and building structures pulling out deceased inhabitants.

The last memory I have with Major Dhatri was in Iraq when we were on our morning run and we can across two young men playing with sticks across the barb wire fence.

The next day we came back and threw two Yankees baseball caps, a pair of baseball gloves and a baseball and played catch over the fence with our bare hands every morning.

Until our squad was deployed to Yemen and after raiding the al-Qaeda headquarters, our helicopter was shot down.

She told me she was proud to know that the father of her children was more heroic than she had thought before.

That he came home and loved his family as much as he did after dealing with all of that.

It takes a special kind of man to endure that kind of

sacrifice as a soldier and still be a father and a husband.

Before I left, she called her daughters downstairs and I prayed with them.

When I was done, I looked out the screen door at the rear of the house and a blue jay was sitting on the railing of the wooden deck.

I saw that as a sign that Dhatri was with us.

I sent a post card with a picture of a blue jay from various parts of the world that I have travelled.

A decade passed and on Christmas I received a post card back from Dhatri's oldest daughter telling me that she had enlisted as a Chaplain's Assistant, and she said that if it had not been for me, she may have grown up resenting the military because of what happened to her father.

No words could describe that feeling.

I have had many successes over the years, but that is the one I am most proud of.

Since then we have created a fund for military families experiencing bereavement, and we have worked together helping military families as well as enlisted men and women around the country and overseas.

Today, she is my assistant, and every day I feel just like I am back on the front lines fighting with Chief Warrant Officer Dhatri and my old crew.

I know Major Dhatri is watching over Blue Jay and I,

as well as our families.

On time.

On target.

Never quit.

"When fear rushed in, I learned how to hear my heart racing but refused to allow my feelings to sway me. That resilience came from my family. It flowed through our bloodline."

-Coretta Scott King

The Author

Paul E. Abbott is a very enthusiastic minister that is infatuated with spiritual development and mental health awareness. Illustrating the importance and impact of foundations forged through faith through fictional literature, films, art, and music in an attempt to raise awareness for the countless organizations and causes around the world that stand to serve.

"It is my dream to write about my experiences through life and intertwine them with divine premises that have the power to influence others and to express the feelings that I have experienced through my journey to educate myself and grow as an individual. It is a pleasure to share this time with all of you, and I pray that this book may influence you to do your part and strive to use the time you have left to leave our world a better place and commit to Forging Foundations for the Future Generations. I pray that you find the courage and become influenced with the willingness to embark on your own path with God and come to love him with all of your heart, mind and soul; and that you come to love your neighbors and every being, man, woman, or child as you would love your own self and your own beloved family. With unconditional love."

This page is dedicated to Veterans who have served in the armed forces and those who are currently serving our country. Thank you for your service and your sacrifices! A special thank you to my cousin Manasseh Arnold who is currently serving in the Army National Guard as well as my cousin Adam Raymond who is currently serving in the Air Force.

"I would say to the House, as I said to those who have joined this government, 'I have nothing to offer but blood, toil, tears, and sweat. We have before us an ordeal of the most grievous kind. We have before us many long months of toil and struggle.' You ask, 'What is our policy' I will say, 'It is to wage war with all our might, with all the strength that God can give us, to wage war against a monstrous tyranny never surpasses in the dark, lamentable catalogue of human crime. You ask, 'What is our aim'. I can answer in one word: 'Victory. Victory at all costs. Victory in spite of all terror. Victory, however long and hard the road may be. For without victory, there is no survival."

- Winston Churchill

100% of the profits from the purchase of this book will be donated to Non-Profit Organizations, Missions, and Churches of All Denominations around the Globe.

I pray that my devotion to create a piece of literature that serves to not only create and/or strengthen individuals relationship with God - but to raise funds and awareness will inspire somebody, or many, to be an answer to a problem.

To bring solutions where there is a need.

To bring healing where there is hurting.

And I pray that when we give our lives to the cause of love and the idea of a world better by it - that even if we are not acknowledged - Our Blessed Lord will be seen through our actions and our sacrifices.

Amen.

Milton Keynes UK
Ingram Content Group UK Ltd.
UKHW020738070124
435550UK00010B/792

NOTES